The Ivory Tower *and* the Smokestack

The Ivory Tower *and* the Smokestack

100 Years of Cooperative Education at the University of Cincinnati

M.B. Reilly

With contributions from Cheryl Cates, Kettil Cedercreutz and E. Sam Sovilla

emmis

books

For further information, contact the publisher at

Emmis Books
1700 Madison Road
Cincinnati, OH 45206
www.emmisbooks.com

Library of Congress Control Number: 2005938758

Cover photo of McMicken tower by Dottie Stover/University of Cincinnati
Designed by Andrea Kupper/Emmis Books

Major funding for this publication was provided by the Herman Schneider Memorial Fund.

Table of Contents

ON THE HILLTOP UNIVERSITY, AN EXPERIMENT MOVES FORWARD IN 1906

Sandy Koufax entered UC's co-op architecture program, actually coming to the university on a basketball scholarship. He also went out for the baseball team, as evidenced by this 1954 photo. And the rest is, clearly, baseball history.

Cooperative education:
The perfect game plan

One-time University of Cincinnati architecture student Sandy Koufax built a career as a superb major league baseball pitcher, a Hall of Famer who won the Cy Young Award three times.

He studied at UC long enough to pitch one season for the Bearcats before turning pro and, in a previously published account, *Tales from Cincinnati Bearcats Basketball*, Koufax partly credits co-op for coaxing him away from his native Brooklyn. "Being out of school half the time sounded good to me," he laughs.

But co-op couldn't quite keep its hold on the man who arguably became history's greatest left-handed pitcher. Instead, with a freight-train of a fastball that audibly *whistled*, Koufax came to tower on the mound, a billboard advertisement for intimidation. In game after game, opposing batters were already down and out as they came up to the plate, and dugout chatter stilled in unwilling homage before the signature buzz of a Koufax fastball.

There was only one obvious way that Koufax's game could be beat: Take away his ever-so-key catchers (Johnny Roseboro and Roy Campanella). If Koufax hadn't had catchers able to handily cope with his bullet pitches, he'd have had to gear down, depriving him of his greatest winning asset. Not to mention that he also had excellent infielders and outfielders backing him up. The point: "No-hitter" and "perfect game" pitcher Sandy Koufax *could not* have achieved greatness all on his own. Indeed, he and his team have been cited, quite literally, as textbook examples of cooperation's perfect players.*

And as in baseball, so it is in business and every other field of play and work. Extraordinary achievement comes from a cooperative group. This truth is the powerful engine that drives cooperative education, which interlocks academic learning with professional experience for students by allowing them to alternate periods of study with paid, professional work. Cooperative education had its global founding at UC in 1906. From an unheralded, unlikely "trial" experiment stubbornly pressed forward by an educational pitchman, the practice has now caught on at more than 1,000 universities in 43 countries.

* The above example is from *Joining Together: Group Theory and Group Skills* by David W. Johnson, professor at the University of Minnesota.

Herman Schneider,
co-op's founder, is born in
Summit Hill, Penn.

First engineering program begins at UC,
then a municipal university.

The cooperative system of education
is proposed at Lehigh University in
Pennsylvania.

1872 — 1873 — 1899

Your money AND Your life: A tale of two co-ops

FIRST, THERE'S THE DRY DEFINITION for the question "What is co-op?" Co-op is the practice wherein students regularly alternate time spent in the classroom with time spent in the workforce as paid professionals. Quite accurate, but not quite the whole story.

It doesn't get at what co-op *really* is for students, their employers and the wider community. Co-op is experience, yes. It's learning and earning, yes. But it's also the priceless intangibles of maturity, growth, responsibility and, most of all, trust. The 100-year story of co-op is a tale of trust fulfilled. It's the thread that runs true throughout co-op history. Co-op students were trusted to help build their city, defend their country and eventually serve around the globe.

At its best, co-op embodies a very personal kind of trust when the young and inexperienced are first handed jobs that mean quite a lot—and sometimes everything—to those around them.

Take, for instance, two co-op students separated by almost a half century: Sam Sovilla, who first co-opped in 1956, and Shannon Walker, who first co-opped in 2003. Sovilla was a sophomore accounting major from West Virginia, "just a big goof-off," as he recalls it, sent without ceremony to downtown Cincinnati to co-op with Mercantile Stores Company, Inc., the parent company of McAlpin's. Walker, of Cincinnati's Clifton neighborhood, first co-opped as a 24-year-old junior in nursing, part of nursing's pilot co-op class.

Sovilla co-opped for $1 an hour, and on his very first morning, he met the

previous co-op student who had held his job. Sovilla got a few pointers and went straight to work. His job that first day? Carrying $37,000 in cash to the bank.

"That was *real* money in those days," Sovilla laughs. Indeed, at the time it represented about 20 years' worth of earnings for him. "What's really funny is that I did it on my very first day before I had filled out any paperwork at Mercantile. Even my co-op advisor at UC barely knew me. I'd just reported to him, and as I stood there during our first meeting, he just called down to Mercantile and said, 'I have your next co-op. I'm sending him down. He'll report by 9 a.m. next Monday morning.' That was it."

Sovilla was also entrusted with the key to the safe, which held about 40 cash boxes. He stuffed all the pay envelopes which, in those days, were filled with cash, not pay*checks*. "I would have tens of thousands of dollars on my desk. It took the whole day to stuff the envelopes, and I couldn't even leave to go to the bathroom unless I found someone specific to stay at the desk for me," he recalls. "But it wasn't till the third day that the

manager even thought to have me fill out any paperwork."

Recent nursing co-op student Shannon Walker, class of 2004, finds herself repeatedly trusted with far more than money. She takes care of lives, and on her very first co-op, which began in June 2003, Walker literally saved a life. She was asked to give a drug closely related to penicillin to a cardiac/pneumonia patient. Having interviewed her patient and knowing that the patient was allergic to penicillin, Walker had doubts about administering the medication as ordered. So, she literally *ran* the hospital hallways to her drug-reference guide, and sure enough, her doubts were confirmed. The related drug about to be administered would cause the same allergic reaction as would penicillin. How serious would that have been? "It's very serious. It could have killed her," explains Walker. "It would have been worse in this situation. The family had just arrived to visit the patient, who could have literally died in front of them."

Walker adds, "I can't tell you how great I felt about it! A mistake was about to be made, and I—the student—was the one who caught it. I was so very proud because someone's life depended on me, and I was able to really come through."

Top: Sam Sovilla as a college student.
Left: Shannon Walker.

Co-op was so closely associated with its founding school and city that the 1934 edition of Webster's Dictionary defined co-op as the "Cincinnati plan."

Geol. Pertaining three divisions of t cludes the Richmond, Lorraine, and Utica formations. — *n.* The Cincinnatian epoch or series. See GEOLOGY, *Chart.* **Cin′cin·nat′i plan** (sĭn′sĭ·nắt′ĭ; *locally often* -nắt′ǎ). *Educ.* The co-operative plan; — originally followed in Cincinnati, Ohio. **cin·cin′nus** (sĭn·sĭn′ŭs), *n.*; *pl.* -NI (-ī). [L., a curl of hair, fr. Gr. *kikinnos*.] A scorpioid cyme. See CYME. — cin

Plan your work and work your plan:
Then, your plan works

In 1906, the world's first class of co-op students
was divided into two sections, and the two groups
alternated places in the classroom and workforce.

Plan your work and work your plan:
Then, your plan works

Who can divorce a river from its source? Just so, we must start at the beginning with Herman Schneider, the founder of modern-day cooperative education.

Schneider once wrote, "It is a good thing for a man to sweat his way to the truth," and he sweated to heave and lift up the new idea of co-op and manhandle it into motion.

The idea of co-op seems pretty tame today. Don't we all know that application is the ever-ready teacher that transforms the underdogs of experience into "upperdogs"? What could be more shrewd and sensible than linking street smarts with textbooks?

But when Schneider proposed co-op, he still lived in the corseted, Edwardian age at the brim between the 19th and 20th centuries. Colleges were intellectual centerpieces perched on hilltops, while industries were rooted in basins and bottoms. Certain boundaries were strapping strong, and most folks *just*

Sketch by an early co-op student, proof of just how often Dean Herman Schneider must have voiced his maxim: "Another way to teach people to swim is by kicking them off the dock."

knew that a good college education was *classical*, based on the English model. Scholars manifestly *did not* sweat.

So upon coming to Cincinnati in 1903, Schneider had already struck out twice, having peddled his revolutionary idea from door to factory door in both Pittsburgh and Bethlehem, Penn. Both cities had rebuffed his educational heresy. Thus, the one-time coal-breaker boy from Pennsylvania resolved to leave home, this time seeking more promising prospects.

At first, he was Wisconsin bound, but at the last minute, he veered off to the industrial center of Cincinnati to accept a casually offered position as an engineering instructor.

It would be prosaic to breezily assert that Cincinnati and its university—then devoted to the liberal arts, with engineering students a fraction of the total population—easily acceded to the wisdom of the new professor's plan. But to speak truth, it was more that Schneider,

UC's College of Engineering is organized.

1901

Herman Schneider arrives at UC from Lehigh University to serve as professor of civil engineering.

1903

Co-op is founded. Beginning on Sept. 24, students in mechanical, chemical and electrical engineering alternate a week at work with a week in the classroom. Dean Schneider coordinates the students' work/school schedules from his home on evenings and weekends.

1906

Upton Sinclair publishes *The Jungle*, a novel exposing the intolerable working conditions in a Chicago slaughterhouse.

Orville and Wilbur Wright are awarded U.S. patent 821,393 for "new and useful improvements in Flying Machines."

who quickly rose to become dean of the UC College of Engineering in 1906, sneakily wedged his cooperative plan in by the academy's ajar back door and then pushed it to a stuttering start.

One fellow academician of the era wrote that Schneider wrung out such queasy permission from the university's board of directors to test-drive his madcap educational contraption that it was akin to their saying, "Let him go ahead. Nothing he can do will harm *that* department."

The co-op proposition squeaked by the UC board with a single vote to spare. All in all, it was a soggy, doubt-laden contract, as evidenced by the wording of the consent: "We hereby grant the right to Dean Schneider to try, for one year, this cooperative idea of education … *[for] the failure of which*, we will not assume responsibility." It was an unringing endorsement if ever there was one, but Schneider quietly delighted in it for the rest of his life. In after years, he publicly preserved the board's painfully reluctant permission on his office wall.

But it was enough. Schneider, an iron-willed optimist—both imaginative idealist and realist—was now off and scheming on how he could make his engineering pipe dream a nuts-and-bolts reality.

He faced a different challenge in persuading students and their families to test his experiment, asking them to gamble their youthful years. At first, the experience-to-education plan meant they would lengthen their college careers by almost two years, and his idea faced the drag that all new ventures do. Too much vision often seems silly. Not enough usually seems sensibly sound.

In the end, Schneider corralled 27 young men to run the co-op gauntlet. It seems he both cajoled and compromised, accepting into the course one Dennis-the-Menace type

who had been "kicked out" of every school he'd attended, a "hopeless" youth who would "wreck" the experiment, according to the boy's own father.

The very first co-op to graduate, George Binns, simply strolled into the program unsuspecting, snared by the dean's personal appeal. Son of an English immigrant family operating a flour mill in Hopkinsville, Ky., the young George Binns had already proved himself at a Kentucky military academy and had won an appointment to the Naval Academy at Annapolis, as much an honor then as now. It seems that while passing through Cincinnati on his way to Maryland, Binns got off the train to visit a friend. This friend was the son of Ernest Du Brul, a leading industrialist in town who was also a member of UC's board of directors. Papa Du Brul mentioned that he had to go to the university to see Dean Herman Schneider. Would the boys like to come along?

They did, and the rest is co-op history, according to George's son, Jack Binns Sr.: "The dean was discussing the nascent co-op program, and he must have been quite the pitch man. At the end of the visit, the dean had really sparked my father's interest and even suggested my father give up his appointment to the Naval Academy and stay in town to try on the new program for size. And my father said, 'By golly, I think I will.'"

Schneider similarly lassoed 12 metal-trade, machine-tool and other local manufacturers into employing pairs of co-op students who would trade off alternating work weeks. Other firms in town remained skeptical so, at first, the dean frankly conspired, worming students into plants. Co-op graduate from the class of 1912, Richard Paulsen, later wrote that, at one point, "It happened that two members of our class wanted especially to work for one machine-tool concern whose president believed that the co-op course was a good thing for

the other fellow. Early in the summer, they got jobs in this plant" with the help of a company employee who had been a college classmate of Dean Schneider.

Both Paulsen and Jack Binns then go on to tell the same story. According to Binns, "The dean met the president of this firm, Frederick A. Geier of what was then Cincinnati Milling Machine, on the train one day. Herman let the cat out of the bag by asking how his co-ops were working out. F.A. said he didn't have co-ops, that the co-op plan would work in some organizations but not his. Herman then had to confess that he'd snuck two in.

"F.A. was pretty angry about the wool being pulled over his eyes, and Herman had to promise that when F.A. got back and checked it out, if the co-ops weren't doing well, Herman would repay all that they'd been given in terms of salary. If they were doing well, F.A. had to accept more co-ops."

Paulsen later recounted, "When the president got back to the plant, he found that these men were in fact on the roll of his employees. He sent for the foreman and asked him about the co-ops. 'Best men I've got,' said the foreman. The president, being a good sport, enjoyed the joke on himself and admitted

It was Dean Schneider's Darwinian custom to put the co-op students to work the summer *before* the start of their freshman year to see if they were made of the right stuff. In co-op's second year, several hundred students applied to the course and about 65 were accepted. Of those, 44 made it through the summer to begin coursework. Once coursework began, these early students were paired off, two students sharing each job. One spent a week at work while his partner was in school. They met on Saturdays to review the workweek and switch roles.

One Connecticut father described his son's initial co-op experience: "To report for work on time, he had to get up at 5:30 a.m., as many other workmen do. It was hot enough to melt lead. The boy was put to filing in the machine-tool room. He did not get back to the college dormitory until nearly six in the evening. Instead of exploring the city or spending a couple of leisurely hours reading or studying, he was glad to tumble into bed by 8:30, tired out. This was a pretty stiff ordeal to ask any boy to undergo. It is. But then I remember my own senior year at college, and the strain of wondering what would come next—whether or not I'd be able to succeed or even earn my living, where and how I could get work. At Cincinnati, in the cooperative courses, that latter worry is done away with. The plunge into practical knowledge about earning a living comes at the beginning, instead of the end."

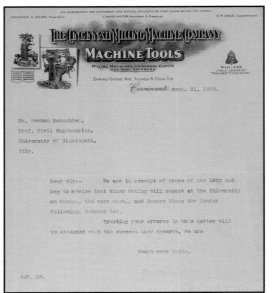

Binn's Mill ~ 1898
with log dam
Christian County, Kentucky

The Binnses operated the first flour mill west of the Alleghenies, according to family lore. And despite his father's hopes, young George Binns, co-op's first graduate, never made it back east over the Alleghenies to go to sea. Instead, he supported himself through college by playing pool in a tavern close to campus. After graduation, Binns went to work at the Cincinnati Milling Machine Co., the company with which he co-opped.

Pictured clockwise are Young George Binns; a letter to Dean Herman Schneider confirming that George Binns and fellow student Elmer Otting would alternate work weeks as co-op students; George Binns' co-op certificate; and a sketch of the Binns family mill.

that this was probably the only way in which he would have started employing co-ops."

Jack Binns remembers it the same way: "When F.A. got back, he called Herman up and said, 'Send me two more co-ops.'"

About 20 years later, this same company—Cincinnati Milling Machine, later renamed Cincinnati Milacron—asked for the entire freshman class in mechanical engineering as co-op students, and the company president publicly acknowledged how wrong he'd been, saying that if the co-op grads were taken from him, his plant would be forced to shut down.

Ralph Flohr (front row, extreme right) was the first co-op student employed by the Cincinnati Lathe & Tool Co. On campus, football player Flohr furthered acceptance of the co-op students, who were looked at somewhat askance since they took their classes apart from the rest of campus. Those early co-op students found it hard to fit in and participate in established extracurricular activities because of their unusual schedules. So, these students formed their own Co-op Athletics Club and fielded the only football team then representing the university. Flohr took up a position as guard, and the 1911 UC yearbook boasts of him, "The same good, old, reliable Flohr. U.C. is fortunate in that Flohr is a co-op and good for two or three more years of hard work. A more consistent man never played the game at U.C." In all, 20 team members were co-op students—and no wonder, as the co-op class was known to play touch football when they were supposed to be in lab.

Co-op Colleges at UC

College of Allied Health Sciences

College of Applied Science

College of Business

Clermont College

College of Design, Architecture, Art, and Planning

College of Engineering

McMicken College of Arts and Sciences

College of Nursing

Raymond Walters College

"We flocked together like sworn brothers"

In a cocky, confident class all their own

The early co-ops might have been "guinea students," but they weren't lab rats. They were known to skip away from the labs to play football on campus grounds while also dodging blackboard exercises. Just ask Arthur Conner from that first co-op class. A classmate recounted, "To illustrate his lecture on gear trains, Professor Jenkins had placed some figures on the blackboard, among them a number of ellipses. It was a warm, spring day, and Arthur, who sat by the window, found the scenery irresistible. Noticing his far-away look, Professor Jenkins inquired suddenly, 'Mr. Conner, what are we talking about?' Arthur gave a quick glance at the oval figures on the board and answered, 'Eggs.' Without a word, Professor Jenkins went to the rear of the room and threw the door wide open, and without a word, Arthur walked out. Then, Professor Jenkins resumed his lecture at the exact point where he had left off."

"All for one and one for all."

—Alexandre Dumas, 1802–1870
French playwright and novelist

"We flocked together like sworn brothers"

Co-op's earliest foot soldiers swaggered through that first academic year. And why not? In their rough, hot co-op labors the summer before the start of their freshman classes, they'd proven they had far more than mere academic fitness.

But, their hard-charging pace—their week-on/week-off course schedule—put them in a class by themselves. They were *in* the university but not quite *of* it. One early student stated, "The first class of freshman co-ops were excluded from all university (extracurricular) activities. A co-op could not indulge in athletics. He was a man without a country, a student without a class." Another added, "Our welcome was as cordial as that of the young man who went to a party (uninvited) and ate just as heartily as if he'd been invited."

By the end of their second year, this hardscrabble co-op crew had had enough. Though greatly outnumbered by the "regular" engineering students and those from other disciplines, the ostracized co-op group organized its own football squad and promptly beat the university's varsity team. Soon, they became the only football team representing the university. Strong because, as 1912 co-op grad Richard Paulsen later wrote, "We flocked together like sworn brothers."

They became a team inside the classroom, too, scraping through and getting into scrapes together. One student described a typical misadventure: "There was one Wednesday afternoon when the whole section of us had a chemistry experiment to perform together. We drew lots and left the unlucky member of the class to look after the apparatus while the rest of us went down to the matinee. As we were turning the corner of Fifth and Walnut in close formation, it was just our luck to run across Professor Frey, who had started us on the experiment an hour before."

Jack Binns Sr. recalls his father, George—the first co-op graduate—scaled new heights when it came to getting into trouble with his fellows. States Jack, "When my father went to school, the old powerhouse was still under construction, but the funnel smokestack of about 200 feet was completed. My father and two other co-ops decided to climb the funnel's interior rail ladder. Another student was first, my father second, and the third behind him. Well, when that first student got to the top and looked over, he passed out—I guess because of the height. He fainted right into my father, and Dad and the other student had to get him down that rail ladder. Dad said it was awful getting him down one rung at a time."

Co-op's challenges and camaraderie were the hallmarks of campus life, such that those pioneering students joked of themselves, "No wonder the co-ops are 'hard boiled' when the profs keep them in hot water so much of the time."

Though the new co-op program isn't advertised, up to 800 students apply for 70 co-op positions.

Two thousand applicants inquire about the co-op program at UC. Fitchburg High School in Fitchburg, Mass. adopts the co-op program, as do public schools in Freeport, Ill.

Cin'cin·nat'i plan (sĭn'sĭ-năt'ĭ; *locally often* -năt'ā). *Educ.* The co-operative plan; — originally followed in Cincinnati, Ohio.

Northeastern University, Boston, is the first university to follow UC in adopting the "Cincinnati plan."

1907 ———————————————— 1908 ———————————————— 1909

Henry Ford introduces the Model T. Its ad slogan is "Gets Ya There, and Gets Ya Back." Cost is $825.

A bright idea

Athletics served the co-op students, helping them to breach the ivory tower. In turn, the co-op students served UC's athletic programs, making national history in some cases. For instance, electrical engineering co-op student Jack Silverman designed a lighting system that made night football games feasible, resulting in America's first night football game. He did all the design work and mounted the floodlights on poles, later saying, "I recall climbing each pole—the poles had steps—to adjust the aim of the lights so that the illumination was uniformly distributed. And, of course, I saw 'the first football game played under electric lights in the United States' in September of that year (1923)."

The legacy was passed down to the next generation. In 1919—more than a decade after Binns, Paulsen and company served as co-op's first "guinea students"—business undergraduates at UC likewise began learning the lessons of labor from the bottom up.

Business student Robert Conrow of the class of 1924 and a handful of other co-op students actually started out well *below* the bottom rung, so to speak. Conrow wrote of a summer co-op in the coal mines of Nellis, W.Va. He termed it his "vacation in the mines," where there wasn't one torture he wasn't exposed to in his first week.

He said, "After being outfitted with working shoes, a miner's cap and lamp, shovel, pick, auger and body piece, tamper, bar, axe, file, powder flask, squibs and can of carbide, we're sent to mine No. 1 to load coal. We have become accustomed to working all bent over … when at the close of day, we just managed to amble home (to the company town), clean up and go to bed, too tired and too sore to eat any supper. If there's any labor harder than shooting and loading coal, you'll want to learn what it is—and stay away from it!"

But he later admitted that his co-op boot camp paid off: "The business end of a sledgehammer, pick and shovel is an excellent position from which to get a proper perspective of the life and problems of those who toil with their hands. Surely, the executive needs this fine art in large measure."

And he and his fellows wouldn't have had it any other way. A co-op contemporary of Conrow humorously adapted this ode to his alma mater:

In Praise of Old UC

St. Peter was showing some new arrivals about the place.

"Here," he said, as he came abreast a happy group shining their halos, "are men who once went to Dennison."

They crossed a daisy-strewn field and saw a number of harpists blithely tuning their instruments. "These men," said St. Peter, "are from Miami."

The strollers crossed an 18-karat paved street, on which faced a jail. Behind the bars were a number of wretched-looking individuals.

"What's the matter with these men?" inquired the newcomers.

"They're from Cincinnati University," replied St. Peter. "If we didn't keep them locked up, they'd go back."

Why climb a smokestack? "I haven't the foggiest."

Why did co-op pioneer George Binns climb UC's smokestack with two fellow students, one of whom fainted at the top? His son, Jack Sr., admits, "I don't know," while just as quickly, grandson Jack Binns Jr. cracks wryly, "Because he was *young* and *male*." Some two decades later, another co-op student, Robert Atkinson, likewise achieved what he calls his most daring student exploit: "Climbing one of the light towers at Nippert Stadium to take photographs from the top platform of the campus and surrounding landmarks with my trusty box camera."

"We flocked together like sworn brothers"

A $13-MILLION IDEA

EARLY IN THE LAST CENTURY, ONE-TIME UC President Charles Dabney sat down to dinner in New York City with steel baron Andrew Carnegie, a mega-industrialist and philanthropist of the time. Of the evening, Dabney later wrote:

"After dining with him (Carnegie) at his house on Fifth Avenue, we were sitting in his library, discussing the problems of engineering education. He was telling me about the great institution he had built for training young men and women in Pittsburgh and its splendid equipment. He was very proud of it. Suddenly, he stopped his narration, turned to me and said, 'Dabney, I hear you have no shops for your engineering college in Cincinnati. How in the world do you get along without them?'

"I explained to him that Cincinnati had a great variety of fine shops representing almost every branch of industry and that we used them. 'How in the world can you do that?' he asked. In reply, I explained to him the method of our cooperative course. He listened intently and after remaining silent for a few moments, turned to me and said, 'Then, you mean to tell me that I have spent $13 millions of dollars in building shops for my school in Pittsburgh when I might have used the shops they already had there?' And, he added, 'And I have had to keep them up to date at great expense; and right now, the president (of Pittsburgh's then Carnegie Institute of Technology) is soliciting me for a million or more to build some more shops. Do you mean to say that I have spent all of this money when I need not have done so?'"

Left: Charles Dabney
Right: Andrew Carnegie

Photos courtesy of Carnegie Mellon University Libraries

Co-op founder Herman Schneider:
He was ever "Co-optimistic"

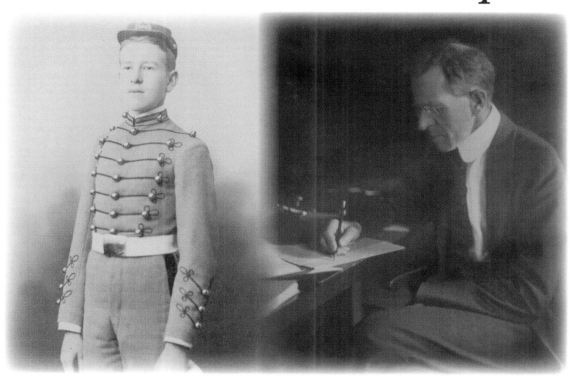

Herman Schneider

Co-op founder Herman Schneider:
He was ever "Co-optimistic"

The straight-laced photos of Dean Herman Schneider belie the warm portrait of him that can be drawn from well-loved tales told by those who remember him.

He reads like a big-gauge Renaissance man—architect, bridge builder, award-winning story writer, essayist, educator, researcher, labor mediator, wartime administrator, art collector and even university president, serving as president of UC from 1929 to 1932. But he never brayed and was happiest and proudest in his modest role as the College of Engineering's first dean, the man who dragged UC from the ivory tower into the world's foundries and factories, mines and machine shops. Yet none of this tells you *who* the man was, *really.*

Schneider's grace, humor, generosity and human foibles still shine through more than 60 years after his death of a heart attack—on the job, of course—on March 28, 1939. His students can always conjure up a choice memory of the man who taught even while serving as dean and who also, in co-op's early years, took responsibility for placing all of his co-op "boys" and visiting them on the job. He invariably invited each student to his house for Sunday evening chat sessions and knew all of them by name.

Dean Schneider was a meticulous man, and it seems he had to be in order to cope with his severe nearsightedness and precarious health, including a hundredfold plague of boils that gave him no rest. But he was always on a quest for original ideas. Once, upon learning how one employer's giant Maltese cat broke up the fatigue and tension of factory work by moving among girls working for a piano manufacturer, Dean Schneider proposed bringing in not a cat, but parrots to the College of Engineering, to break the monotony of work for students. But a realistic colleague pointed out what the first result would be. "Thereupon," said a colleague, "the dean's enthusiasm for parrots faded."

University of Pittsburgh adopts co-op.

George Binns becomes UC's first co-op graduate. Co-op is adopted at the University of Detroit.

Co-op is adopted at the Georgia Institute of Technology and by the Rochester Institute of Technology. At UC, the first co-op class graduates.

◄——————— 1910 ——————————————— 1911 ——————————————— 1912 ———————►

The Boy Scouts of America is incorporated.

The first long-distance automobile race in Indianapolis is won by Ray Harroun. The average speed in the race is 74.4 mph, and one driver is killed.

Standard Oil establishes America's first gas station in Cincinnati.

A one-time student, John Johnson was sure he was going to have to drop out of school when his father died unexpectedly during the Depression. Johnson went to the dean's office and informed the secretary that he would be leaving the program. The secretary told him to return in a few hours to meet with the dean. "The dean told me that my grades made me qualified for a scholarship tuition loan," Johnson says. "He also said the people in Cincinnati had made funds available to him to help students who needed financial assistance for living expenses. He then handed me a $50 check.

"I had the opportunity to see the dean as a very warm, caring person," Johnson adds. "He was efficient, prepared, knew my needs and had a logical plan."

John Abel, a business administration student who graduated in 1944, had similar recollections dating back to the Depression. He believes that the dean made it possible for him to stay in school. "Dean Schneider was a good customer of my grandfather's shoe store where I was working to earn money for tuition," Abel states. "The dean arranged it with my grandfather so that I could work full time and go to school full time. So, working for my grandfather became my co-op job."

Above: Herman Schneider, age 5, standing at right. Seated at left is his brother, Anton Schneider, age 7. Both attended Lehigh University in Pennsylvania, and Anton then went on to build bridges throughout the U.S., subway tunnels in New York City and railroads in the Andes.

As for Herman (shown left in uniform), his schoolboy military training at a Chester, Penn., academy stayed with him throughout a lifetime of tick-tock habits during which he transformed UC into the West Point of co-op. One friend recalled that Herman placed a chair in a proscribed position at the head of his bed every night. Every article of clothing he needed for the next day was placed upon it, the positioning for which "would not vary by a fraction of an inch from one year's end to the next. He could arise in absolute darkness and dress without loss of a single motion."

Herman and his wife, Louise Bosworth Schneider

Herman Schneider was so nearsighted, he couldn't recognize his wife across the table without his glasses. He was also definitely *not* a morning person. His fun-loving wife made it a regular practice to engage him in conversation at breakfast. His replies often came out muddled and mixed. For instance, Schneider was teased long afterward when, having to meet his wife's relatives coming in on an early-morning train, he gravely asked the gateman, "On what train will the track from Cleveland come in?"

Another alum, Marguerite Whitney, a 1938 graduate of the business program, has the sweetest memories of Dean Schneider. While a student, Whitney co-opped in the dean's office for two summers, assisting the executive secretary. Recalls Whitney, "I can still picture Dean Schneider. He would go up to Michigan in the summers to vacation, but he always left ice-cream money for the office staff. I was married (to Carl Whitney, a 1930 electrical engineering grad), and my husband had a job. So, I was the one in the office who had a car. It was my job to make a run to Graeter's over on McMillan for ice cream. I always had all these orders to fill. I can still remember that Barb Kiessling, the registrar, always had one dip of chocolate and one dip of peach."

Whitney further insists that this ice cream was no luxury but a necessity. "We *needed* it because it was always so hot in the summers in Baldwin Hall! We didn't have air conditioning. I can't even recall that we had a fan. We'd pull the shades down to keep the sun out, but that meant no air flow. I remember working one Saturday till 4 p.m. when we had to get some letters out. It was 104 degrees that day."

When pondering how she got the ice cream back to the office without a meltdown, Whitney laughs, "I don't know anymore. Maybe I was the only one who had ice cream, and everyone else had ice milk?"

Such recollections wax hot and cold on Dean Schneider. Marie Seuberling Ludeke, a business graduate from 1940, also worked as a secretary at UC from 1935–40. She recalls that Dean Schneider always walked. He would never drive because of his weak eyesight. The young secretary and her brother would often stop to give the dean a ride to work when they spotted him at the bottom of University Avenue where the No. 35 streetcar dropped him off. And no matter how cold the winter morning, Dean Schneider would always roll down all the windows in the car.

Similarly, he always rode on the open back end of the city's streetcars. It seems that after enduring the threat of consumption and a case of malaria when he was young, Schneider was germ phobic and always glad to seek fresh air, which, in his opinion, guaranteed a "germ-free" environment. Whatever his reasons, Ludeke was just grateful for one thing: "On winter mornings, I was glad it was a short ride!"

Co-op founder Herman Schneider: He was ever "Co-optimistic"

RETREAT AND ADVANCE:
WORLD WAR I AND ITS AFTERMATH

Cincinnati goes to war

The U.S. officially entered World War I in April 1917, and Cincinnati crowds gathered to celebrate a fundraising victory in June of that year. Within a week's time, the city had raised more than $1 million for Red Cross relief efforts. Here, two leading businessmen—at least one of whom was a co-op employer—paint over previous fundraising milestones to celebrate meeting their million-dollar mark.

Below: Student troops assemble on UC's football field.

"You can do anything with bayonets except sit on them."

—*Count Camillo Benso di Cavour, 1810–1861*
Italian statesman

Camp khaki:
Co-op stands down

The U.S. entry into the First World War upended the co-op program, which was suspended from September 1918 to early 1919 as virtually every male student not already enlisted—and remember that engineering and co-op were still all-male at this time—became a soldier in the Students' Army Training Corps (SATC). Time once devoted to co-op was now committed to military exercises as the university redesigned its wartime curriculum. Co-op students not only studied engineering but took a stab at military tactics, too. Troops of students drilled and marched on Clifton Avenue, training with real bayonets, a practice that was later discontinued.

It's easy to imagine why, given the recollections of chemical engineering student Michael Colncurcio, who drilled at UC just after the war: "I have a scar on my leg to show for it, the result of dorm students playing with the bayonets—throwing them like a knife to stick into the ground. One of the bayonets struck a stone below the surface of the ground and ricocheted, hitting my leg."

You're in the Army now
Unpainted wooden barracks went up in about a month's time, some of them standing where Swift Hall, the Steger Student Life Center and Tangeman University Center are now. The 13 barracks were christened "Camp Cincinnati" and housed nearly 1,000 UC students who voluntarily signed on for the Students' Army Training Corps as privates in the U.S. Army. They were subject to military discipline, required to march in formation between classes and attended class under strict supervision—no skipping allowed. They received Army pay and lived in the campus barracks even if they were Cincinnati residents. The student-soldiers' bedding was hung out to air every Tuesday morning and a healthy gargle was the routine of each morning.

UC's College of Engineering begins its art collection with a $500 gift from the senior class.

UC's co-op enrollment stands at 473 while employers number 86.

While co-op is suspended at UC so that students can train in the Students' Army Training Corps of World War I, Marquette University begins co-op with 175 students.

←————— 1916 —————————————— 1917 ————————————————— 1918 —————→

The U.S. Army founds the Reserve Officer Training Corps (ROTC).

America enters World War I on April 6.

World War I ends.

Henry Ford awards equal pay to women.

Co-ops in wool uniforms

One-time co-op student Edward Wilson likened the wearing of these military uniforms to "torture." He so hated them that he later set up a scholarship for co-op students so that those unable to afford school would, at the very least, *not* have to join the Reserve Officer Training Corps (ROTC) in order to study engineering. "I was *extremely* allergic to wool," Wilson recalled. "During our freshman year, we wore a World War I wool uniform with choke collar and spiral, wrap-around leggings. I really do not know how I got through the first year, especially the summer."

Campus armed for war, and barracks sprouted all over UC. Nearly 2,000 more young men—in addition to the regularly enrolled students—swelled the campus ranks, coming to live and learn the electrician's and auto mechanic's trades. Even Dean Herman Schneider took a leave of absence from the university to serve in Washington, D.C., in the Ordnance Department.

That's not to say that student life stood still during the war years. Student soldiers were still at ease to enjoy campus traditions, like cherished football rivalries. One-time English faculty member Clyde Park recalled the day a co-op student-turned-soldier named Harry Pockras strode through his open office door: "I first met him on the day before Thanksgiving in 1918. Late in the afternoon, a chap in Army uniform introduced himself and produced exactly 100 $1 bills. His

company of SATC soldiers had raised a fund to back the UC football team against Miami. He was afraid to risk keeping the money in the barracks overnight and hoped to find a member of the faculty who would take care of it. I placed the greenbacks in my desk between two bundles of somewhat less valuable reports. The next day, Private Pockras called for the money and later made the distribution called for by a tie score."

As the thunderclap of the Great War passed in 1919, co-op revived and advanced, mandatory now for both engineering and business students. Private Pockras took up a new post as the first editor of a just-founded co-op magazine known as *The Co-Operative Engineer*. And for the first time, women came marching into the co-op camp.

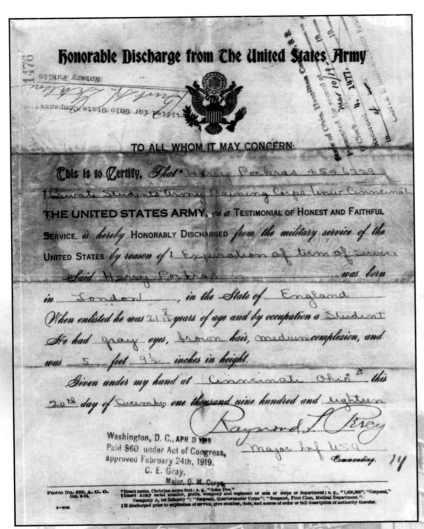

As the Students' Army Training Corps discharge papers prove, co-op students like Harry Pockras (above right) went out of the Army and into a changed future. New endeavors began, and doors opened all over campus, including those of Memorial Hall, the university's first dorm, named in remembrance of the war's dead. As the only available residence for men, it housed mostly out-of-town co-op students. Chemical engineering student Michael Colncurcio stated, "When the men's Memorial dormitory opened, I was one of the first occupants. We had a lot of fun in the original dorm. The students had been living singly or in pairs in private homes, and we all appreciated the fellowship and friendship afforded by dorm contacts."

These UC students were photographed during their last day on campus, before going east to the ships that would take them to the Marne and Argonne Forest. While the war siphoned young men from campus, at least one later co-op student came to UC *because* of the war. Harold Senf, '25 civil engineering grad, first learned about UC as a sailor during the war. "At a rap session at sea, we discussed what we hoped to do after being discharged from service. I said that I had a tuition scholarship at Cornell University, but a shipmate mentioned the co-op course at UC." After his 1919 discharge, Senf enlisted in the co-op course, opting for UC over Cornell.

The '20s that roared:
The women come marching in

In 1920, the University of Cincinnati admitted women to the co-op program—the first college in the world to do so. The pioneering women labored under the nickname of "co-eps" and even "co-opettes."

In back, from left to right, are Ruby Schoen, Charlotte Atherton, Ruth McFarlan and Margaret Maynard. Seated in front are, from left, Kathryn Gillis, Helen Norris and Myrtle Hay.

"I was taught that the way of
progress is neither swift nor easy."

—Marie Curie, 1867–1934
Chemist and pioneering investigator of radioactivity

The '20s that roared:
The women come marching in

In 1920, no school in the United States yet admitted women into preparatory programs for engineering. Herman Schneider and UC changed all that, thanks to a young Cincinnatian named Ruth McFarlan and her aunt, Anna McFarlan.

The aunt, it happens, was acquainted with Dean Schneider's secretary, Anna Teasdale, and asked Teasdale to approach the dean on behalf of young Ruth who wanted to study engineering. The upshot: Come fall 1920, seven young women—with shoulders broad enough to bear the sobriquet of "co-eps" and even "co-eppettes," as they were called—entered the UC co-op course as either chemical engineering or commercial engineering (business) students, the only two programs pried open for them in the College of Engineering.

These women—and those who followed them—couldn't skirt the challenges they faced in braving the stronghold of gears, grease and manhood. Of these seven original girl "gearheads," four stayed the course while three eventually opted out—Charlotte Atherton opened a tea room with her mother, Ruby Schoen transferred to the liberal arts program and Margaret Maynard married.

One 1924 male contemporary of the co-eps sketched this cartoon and admitted that "the girls were very coldly received by both employers and co-workers." He went on to condescendingly offer his support with an appeal to his fellows: "Be considerate of the co-eps. If you find a vanity case in your can of Crisco, understand that some poor chemical co-ep was awkward for the first day of work. (And be sure to return the misplaced article, for the poor dear is lost without her powder.) And if you feel more or less poisoned after eating a salad in a certain large cafeteria, consider that some poor 'Nutrition' [a co-ep in the nutrition program] has not yet learned to differentiate between mayonnaise and silver polish. Die if you must, but please do not blame the co-ep."

The reality, according to Mary Blood, who entered the chemical engineering program in 1921, was something quite different. Yes, she and her women classmates packed Crisco during early morning hours at a Procter & Gamble factory. They also hauled lumber and became handy with crowbars too.

Co-op resumes at UC, now as a mandatory program for all engineering and business students. Elsewhere, co-op begins at Drexel University and at MIT.

UC becomes the first school in the country to admit women into the co-op program. Also that year, UC becomes the envy of the Ivies as Harvard University adopts co-op. One-time UC co-op Charles Lytle, '13, directs the newly established Department of Industrial Co-Operation at Harvard.

At UC, a mandated hobby hour begins for co-op students. Hobby activities include chess, band, a literary society, a wireless radio club, sketching, baseball, basketball, boxing, wrestling, tennis and track.

◄———— 1919 ———————————————— 1920 ———————————————— 1921 ————►

"There she is. ..." The first Miss America is crowned not in Atlantic City but in New York City. The first winner was found not to be a "Miss" but a "Mrs." and the mother of two children.

U.S. women receive the right to vote with ratification of the 19th amendment.

Earle Dickson, a cotton buyer for the Johnson gauze bandage company, devises a ready-made, sterile bandage strip for his accident-prone bride.

First co-ep club

The co-eps thrived, building their numbers from seven to 22 in only three years; however, life wasn't easy. Anna Bartruff, who had her first co-op work experience in 1927, recalled making $13.20 a week as a production clerk for Remington Rand in Norwood. Unfortunately, she admitted, "We were docked 20 minutes for any tardiness. I was tardy often since I rode two or three streetcars to get there. I made $8.97 for Thanksgiving week [in 1927] since we were not paid for the holiday, and I was [so] often tardy."

Top row, from left, are Elizabeth Schwebel, Catherine Leyman, Martha Robbins, Miriam Palmer, Ruth Shepard, Isolina Brandenburgh, Marie Heintz. Middle row, from left, are Ethel Wise, Elaine Wenzel, Dorothy Wolf, Kathryn Gillis, Rosemary Norris, Elizabeth Earls and Winifred Brown. Bottom row, from left, are Rachel Wolf, S.E. Conover, Mildred Wagner, Ruth McFarlan, Catherine Betz, Helen Norris, Margaret Bachler and Gertrude Geldreich.

Ruth McFarlan, Helen Norris, Myrtle Hay and Kathryn Gillis persevered in the co-op course, graduated in 1925 and went into the work world. Regrettably, McFarlan died within five years of earning her degree. Gillis became a private secretary at Pogue's Department Store (where she had co-opped). Hay, a chemical engineering grad, went to work at Rollman's, a department store. Meanwhile, Norris, who also earned a chemical engineering degree, found so few doors open to her in the industry that she later returned to campus to earn advanced degrees and eventually taught at UC.

Though armed with education, these women graduates faced long odds. During their years at UC, they found that firms employing male co-op students refused to consider women. And even with diplomas in hand, women had to contort themselves to fit a particular mold. One 1937 employer paradoxically sought a woman worker who "must be an attractive young woman, a girl who has had a considerable amount of experience."

So strong were the social, cultural, educational and workplace restrictions binding women that by 1946, only 13 women had actually earned engineering degrees from UC. In large part, the numbers remained small because it wasn't until 1943, under the exigencies of World War II, that UC accepted women into *all* of its engineering courses.

"I'm convinced that UC women are here only to get a man."

Cartoon from a 1949 edition of the UC *News Record*
Dismissal of women's academic role and their contributions was part of an enduring legacy. Leo Wilcox, one of the first African Americans to enter co-op (in 1953 in his case), laughs at himself now when he looks back and admits how surprised he was to see women co-ops in the engineering program. "During our first week, a lot of us engineering students were gathered for convocation. I saw a couple of girls in the crowd, and I remember thinking, 'What are *they* doing here?! Engineering is for *men*.' It's amazing, but I really thought that at the time!"

Fourth from left in this photo of secretaries in the College of Engineering is Anna Teasdale, who served as Dean Herman Schneider's secretary from 1911 onward. She played the role of intermediary in advocating for the entry of women into co-op.

The first women students in the co-op program took the same courses as men, except for a few highly technical courses in mechanics and metallurgy, for which cultural studies were substituted. Co-eps entering in 1921 included one named Mary Blood, a chemical engineering student. Wrote Blood, "We like the feeling of being pioneers. It would be somewhat nicer if there were more of us, but then, it seems that the enthusiasm makes up for the present lack of numbers."

Above, from left are co-ep pioneers Ruby Schoen, Helen Norris, Ruth McFarlan and Margaret Maynard.

In 1925, these women made history by graduating from the College of Engineering and Commerce, as it was called at the time. Just a year before in 1924, one of their male classmates wrote, "Courage is the chief virtue of the comparatively unknown co-ep. They certainly have earned it (their degrees) after their long struggle against many handicaps, not the least of which was public opinion."

From left, Helen Norris, Kathryn Gillis and Ruth McFarlan.

WOMEN IN CO-OP: STEPCHILDREN IN INDUSTRY RECALLING THEIR FIRST 50 YEARS

IN 1934, HELEN NORRIS MOORE looked back to her days as one of the original seven women who busted gender barriers by "crashing" the co-op program. She wrote of her memories in *The Co-Operative Engineer.*

One co-ep's journey

But what of those early days? They were much the same as they are now. We felt as you probably do now regarding the many quizzes and lab experiments. Physics was hard, parts of chemistry easy. Such thoughts as these ran through our heads—"What good are all these reports? When will we ever be finished? How long will this job last? Will I ever get a raise? I wish we had an afternoon off to go to a show like the Liberal Arts people." And then, suddenly, we were seniors.

Then we were graduates looking for the ever-elusive job. ... In the first place, women were not so desirable in chemical industries, and in the second place, I had tacked a Mrs. to my name. Somehow or other, those two conditions made things rather difficult. Even having the identical training as a man, the man is always preferred. He may be somewhat of a dub and the woman quite brilliant, but the man is chosen. Occasionally, the employer will take a chance [if] the woman agrees to accept a few dollars a week less. A lucky chemical may get a job doing routine analysis in the laboratory of some chemical plant. The duties of answering the telephone, caring for the filing system and even washing the luncheon dishes are very apt to be added. I was acquiring my experience in this manner, when just as I was fed up with doing magnesium determinations ... somehow fate stepped in with the chance to do graduate work. Fine! I started school again, but what a difference! I studied now, really studied for learning's sake. Then came the best offer yet—an instructorship in my department ... actually teaching!

MARY LOU BRUECKNER FOLLOWED IN Helen Norris Moore's footsteps some 30 years later and wrote similarly of her experiences as a gal gearhead in 1958.

"What the heck are you doing in engineering?"

Without the aid of a slide rule, I estimate my having been asked this question at least one hundred times in the last two years. On every Registration Day, I am met with the now-familiar query, "Are you still here? I thought you would be married by this time." One of these fateful days, I'm going to brush aside the restrictions placed on me by my convent upbringing and utter, "What the #@*! do you care?" Of course, that will ruin the impression I've made of being a good-natured, sweet co-ed who had mistakenly stood in the wrong line on registration day. I suppose it will show me for what I really am—a normal, happy-go-lucky girl with a shattered sense of humor.

I have found, through personal experience, the following to be sound advice for all potential women engineers:

1. Start off in the right line on Registration Day.

2. Learn how to eliminate blushing.

3. Come prepared with a reply to the question: "What the heck are you doing in engineering?"

IN 1975, LINDA WALLACE, '79, ECHOED back to Helen Norris Moore when writing about her co-op experiences at Cincinnati Milacron, Inc.

Alone at lunch

There was a certain amount of social isolation caused by me being the only woman in the department. Men and women rarely ate lunch at the same table. Generally, the (secretarial) women worked together, knew each other well and ate together at lunch. The (professional engineer) men did likewise. This put me in an awkward position. Though the men were friendly in the office, I did not feel entirely welcome at their lunch table. Yet I did not know any of the women, and they usually had different lunch hours than I.

Most puzzling was the attitude of some of the women toward me. One of the secretaries was consistently reluctant to help with my work although she was always eager to help the men. Another woman, who apparently assumed I was incapable of doing my own work, asked if I enjoyed my job of tracing the men's drawings.

The original co-eps reunite
From left, front row, Charlotte Atherton Driskell, Ruby Schoen Lucas, Kathryn Gillis. Back, from left, Margaret Maynard Cook, Helen Norris Moore and Myrtle Hay Suit.

Two of the above women came back to UC during their working careers. By the time this photo was taken in 1955, Margaret Maynard Cook was an artist in UC's Medical College, and Helen Norris Moore was teaching in the botany and bacteriology department at UC.

These women were barrier benders, facing down challenges throughout their lives. Following in their footsteps were co-eps like Wanda Mosbacker, '34, who still recalls her first job after graduation, working as the supervisor of women's stepployment at a large corporation. She says, "I'll tell you how I got equitable salaries for women past the assistant treasurer who was a real chauvinist. I would double their (women employees') recommended salary increases and then he'd halve them, and so they'd get a fair increase."

The co-op curriculum:
An art-full course

Dean Herman Schneider laid out his day as meticulously as he laid out his clothing every evening. He devoted a rigid unit of time to each activity or project and then moved on when that time was up—no matter what. He expected his students to do the same, as evidenced by this student sketch of co-op life. One co-op student of the period recalled how co-op students didn't quite cut loose after a week's worth of classes and study: "As soon as classes were over at 12:30 p.m. on Saturday, most of us teamed up and studied right through until early Sunday morning when we went up to one of the many biergartens, bierstubes or rathskellers for a beer."

The co-op curriculum:
An art-full course

Those early co-op classes were distilled exertion, frank endurance tests for the hard driving. Each student conformed to a rigorous discipline. The Schneider students in engineering and, later, business and design were literally scheduled to be in the classroom from 8:30 in the morning to 5 in the evening, plus half-days, at least, on Saturday. The nights were for study.

Ninety-four-year-old Marguerite Whitney ticks off a litany of classes she took under Herman Schneider's co-op scheme—ancient history; chemistry and a lab; geology and field trips; accounting with a lab; business law; economics; literature; art, art history and field trips; statistics and geography.

Another former Schneider student, Wanda Mosbacker, recalls, "We had ten minutes between classes. If you wanted, you had just enough time to run into the bumming room at the foot of the stairs on the first floor of Baldwin Hall. That was our lounge. You could have just enough time for a hand of bridge. It was a convenient place to keep your books so you didn't have to carry them all day."

She continued, "We took business and design courses, engineering, science and some liberal arts courses. I took

The sketcher sketched and the chess mates checked, all while the band played on
A sketching class captured these scenes of fellow students during hobby hour. The hobby hour orchestra included both students and faculty and was led by Karl Wecker of the Cincinnati Conservatory of Music.

UC co-op students begin a new system—alternating one month on the job with one month in school.

The first Co-op Day is held. It becomes an annual event through 1953, allowing students to exhibit their accomplishments.

— 1925 ————————— 1926 ————————— 1927 →

President Calvin Coolidge gives a speech saying, "... the chief business of the American people is business. ..."

Ty Cobb hits for the 4,000th time in his career.

The era of talking pictures arrives with *The Jazz Singer.*

True to its co-op roots, the UC Marching Band requires hardy members. It's a decades-long tradition that the band enters Nippert Stadium to perform at halftime by running full tilt down the long steps from the top lip of the stadium to the field below, all while dressed in full regalia and toting their instruments. Said one later co-op band member, Ed Irvin, "I always remember trying not to trip running down the steps at Nippert." Because former band director Bob Hornyak had a half-serious rule: "If anyone fell, you had to roll them out of the way so they wouldn't interfere with the next person."

The hobby hour band marked the start of what would become UC's Marching Band. The first rehearsal in 1920 attracted only eight co-op students. One of them was Ralph Van Wye, '24, who had played in an Army band during World War I. Of that inauspicious start, Van Wye was heard to joke, "The only letter we could form was the letter 'I.'"

One later co-op, Edward Irvin, says, "The camaraderie in the band is unique. You're all working to create something beautiful. It's a camaraderie similar to that of co-op. You share a class schedule with a very small group, and that helped us form very close, lifelong friendships."

psychology, journalism and calculus in the evening, too. It was a good thing I was a night person. We studied late at night.

We normally carried 28 credit hours. (Fifteen is considered a full schedule today.) *This* was the course as designed by Dean Schneider."

Added to every day's academic blend was a mandated "hobby hour" at noon. The military-trained dean had designed a break that was no "brake" for his students.

Since the daily regimen of his students was a continuous procession from one class to another with just time enough for lunch before a solid afternoon of studio or laboratory work, Schneider commanded a noontime change of pace for the "brain-fagged co-op" wherein students, in order to relax, were paradoxically asked to take on one more thing.

High noon meant high engagement in anything that would provide them a marked change of gait—sketching, orchestra or band, language and literature gatherings, chess, horseshoes, fencing, basketball and more.

These hobbyists ended up emulating their hard-driving dean. The musicians arranged regular orchestral performances, the hobby hour band began performing at UC's football games, while sports teams organized tournaments.

Charging down the steps "was only scary the first time; the second time, you were used to it," recalls co-op band member Edward Irvin. "I thought it was just neat from the beginning. The crowd would trash talk us, saying, 'When you goin' to fall?' In the whole first year, I only saw one person fall, and he fell sideways into the crowd which caught him. So, fortunately, it didn't start a domino effect. It was an exciting time, and we really built the excitement with our war whoop as we ran down those steps."

Edward Irvin in band uniform, taken Oct. 29, 1966, when Irvin was a freshman.

Herman Schneider was a poet, well-regarded short-story writer, amateur painter and sculptor. In fact, he was named class poet when a senior at Lehigh University. Photographed here in his office, Schneider is flanked by two paintings given to the university by graduating students.

It's clear that Schneider—worker, poet, painter and sculptor—was seeking to engrave his own eclectic appreciation for utility and beauty upon his students. An avid reader and admirer of Asian philosophy and art, Schneider also wanted students to broaden themselves by visiting area art museums. The students protested that their heavy school and work duties prevented them from such excursions. Undeterred, Schneider then began the custom of collecting great art and hanging it in the school's corridors, lobbies and landings, thus transforming the engineering halls into art galleries. Students took up the practice, each class raising funds to purchase a gift of art for the school at graduation time, providing the foundation for the university's well-respected art collection.

UC's College of Engineering began collecting art in 1916, thanks to fundraising efforts by students, who often turned to Dean Herman Schneider to advise them on purchases. The art collection grew rapidly with alumni and friends also making donations, including this Edgar Degas sketch donated by Mr. and Mrs. Charles Taft. The work is titled *Ballerina Adjusting Her Stocking*, capturing the immediacy of a moment as a solitary dancer gracefully arranges her outfit before a performance.

Winter, painted in 1882 by Edwin Abbey, was a gift of the engineering class of 1923. The work is evidence of the influence of Impressionism that marked Abbey's watercolors of the time. Philadelphia-born, it's possible that Abbey painted *Winter* during a visit to New York.

Having grown up in Pennsylvania's anthracite coal region, Dean Herman Schneider must have particularly appreciated *Coal Miner*, less a portrait than a character study with its frank depiction of the intense effects of hard labor and harsh conditions on the face of the subject. By Herman Henry Wessel, an Indiana-born artist who studied in the U.S. and Europe, *Coal Miner* was painted about 1910 and was a gift to UC from the class of 1920.

INSTABILITY AND CHANGE:
THE GREAT DEPRESSION AND WORLD WAR II

The Great Depression, which defeated millions of Americans who drifted around the country hungry and begging, had strung itself out for nearly ten years when this photo was taken in the heart of downtown Cincinnati in October 1938.

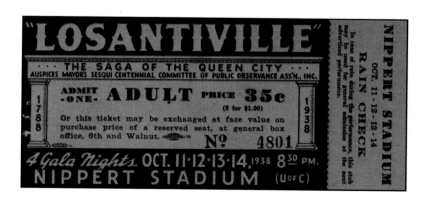

Opera and shows were provided in UC's Nippert Stadium for a few years, and Depression-era co-op student Robert Atkinson recalls how he saved on the cost of admission: "It was easy to use the performers' entrance and then take a seat in the audience."

> *"There is no education like adversity."*
>
> —*Benjamin Disraeli, 1804–1881*
> *English statesman and novelist*

Occupation:
Unemployed

As the Great Depression wrung out the 1930s, at least a quarter of the nation was stranded in unemployment lines that unraveled to impossible lengths, snaking around the same blind corners year upon year. Three quarters of those who *had* jobs were working part-time—short hours laced with vulnerability. And up to seven million young people between the ages of 16 and 25 were out of school, out of work, and mostly, just plain out of luck.

The Depression brutalized this nation, and in the curdling market cycle, the battered co-op program openly choked.

Sunk in the Depression
Cincinnatians turned a crater just north of Gest Street into a fishing hole—quite successfully for some, as evidenced by this 1930 photo, at left, of a broadly smiling local who obviously netted a bonanza. The unknown photographer typed "The Champion" beneath the image.

Herman Schneider becomes president of UC, a post he reluctantly holds till 1932, when he returns to his beloved engineering college and co-op program. Also, UC begins a cooperative course in aeronautical engineering.

UC has 1,800 co-op students and more than 300 employers. Schools across the nation, including medical and divinity schools, have adopted the co-op plan, as have schools in England, Germany, China and Hawaii.

— 1928 ——————————— 1929 ——————————— 1930 —

On Wall Street, stock prices climb in wild speculation.

The stock market crashes, and America enters the Great Depression.

The first cartoon with sound features Felix the Cat.

More than 1,300 banks fail in the United States.

Before graduation in 1932, student William Wenzel took on an extracurricular job—repossessing cars, a booming trade in hard-luck times. The proper way to repossess a car in those days—with a legal writ—cost $35. "So, we stole them," he admits. "One of my fraternity brothers, Woody, would locate the car and back up and hook on a tow rope. I sat in the car and steered while he towed it through traffic. This worked all right in Ohio, but when we crossed the bridge to Kentucky, we found the authorities unsympathetic. As a result, Woody spent some nights in jail."

Other co-ops just opted to build their own cars instead. Above, from left are William Thompson, Charlotte Gross, Ned Drucker, Allen Lloyd and Lea Klein Sachs. Lloyd and Thompson—along with Cliff Garrett—designed and built the car as a senior mechanical engineering project in 1934. The chassis, engine and power train were from a Model A Ford. The students designed the body using biplane wing parts, hoops from iron water pipes and a skin of sheet iron. Lloyd later wrote, "We had only minimum time for testing after making it roadworthy, but as I remember, we made one road test of 32 miles per gallon at city driving speed. I do recall a nice spring day when we test drove it to Oxford, but I don't think we impressed any co-eds there."

For his first co-op in 1931, business student Ned Ackner, pictured at left as a senior, partnered with fellow student George Alcoke to run a root beer stand at the corner of Glenway and Warsaw avenues in Western Hills. "We ran it every day of the summer from noon to 10 p.m. We set up in a parking lot and had to mix the root beer ourselves, a mix of syrup and sugar, which we then carbonated via coils that ran through an ice box to cool the liquid. During rush hour in the late afternoon, I could draw four mugs at one time," Ackner recalls. "We were at a Western Hills hub, and business was hopping. We gave complimentary mugs to children and to the two cops who patrolled that area."

But even hobbled as it was by events, UC's team co-op did rally, literally becoming drivers toward a more prosperous future. For instance, fueled by urgency, faculty packed students into cars, caravanning to factories throughout Ohio. Whenever they found a job, they left a student to take it.

Co-op became a lifeline yanked hard and stretched tense to meet the ongoing crisis. New forms of "co-op" had to be engineered—baby-sitting and grading papers, manning candy stands and "jerking sodas," fighting forest fires as well as building mountain roadways, and even black-topping the network of short-cut footpaths worn across campus lawns.

One-time architecture student Jim Alexander, '40, tells how the National Youth Administration provided funds to actually hire co-op students to pave campus footpaths. "Some of us speculated that if we picked out a prominent spot in the campus lawn and repeatedly tramped down the grass in, say, a 30-foot diameter circle leading nowhere…that when we returned to school after the next co-op, we would find a neatly blacktopped 18-inch-wide circular walkway," he states. "Years later, when I returned as a teacher (to UC), I named one of those narrow, but carefully blacktopped, little paths that was connecting two concrete sidewalks. I called it the Norwood Lateral."

Similarly, Joseph Mancini, a 1935 aeronautical engineering grad, later wrote, "I remember one occasion, because I needed money so badly, [co-op placement officer Calvert Messinger] got me a baby-sitting job. After I had gotten the two young people to bed that night, I fell asleep on the davenport, and when the couple arrived about two in the morning, they did not have their key, and they had a very hard time awakening me. When I finally did wake up, they were furious with me. They were so mad, they gave me $1 for the evening and made me walk home. It was quite a ways from campus, and it took me two hours to walk home to my own bed. That was the last of my baby-sitting experiences."

Mancini later co-opped as a laborer cleaning petrified

Co-op students Raymond Bisplinghoff, '40, left, and A.C. Ballauer, '38, assembling an airplane at Aeronica (Aeronautical Corp. of America) at Lunken Airport in 1936. Bisplinghoff later joined the aerospace engineering faculty at the Massachusetts Institute of Technology while Ballauer became a project engineer at McDonnell Aircraft Corp. in St. Louis.

meat off sausage-making equipment and old packing-house machinery for the Cincinnati Butcher Supply Co. Other co-op jobs later had him hitchhiking to and from a DuPont Co. machine shop in Tennessee, selling Christmas savings accounts for a local bank and even hawking Sunday afternoon airplane rides at $5 a pop for Italian nobility— a count and a marchese who owned three airplanes at Cincinnati's old Hughes Airport.

"I would have to hitchhike from Cincinnati to Old Hickory, Tenn., which would take me two days going and two days returning. It was very hard to get work. It was practically impossible to get anything related to my aeronautical engineering degree. This gives you some idea of how tough things were. Upon graduation, I was broke and owed the university money and needed a job desperately."

In 1932, almost three years into the Depression, the Queen City Tire Co. on Harrison Avenue sold a quart of oil for 17 cents and a gallon of gas for 18 cents.

Similarly, William Wenzel, 1932 civil engineering grad, became a bus driver—with absolutely no training under his belt, nor under his lead foot. He started out as a mere bus company ticket agent at UC. He took orders by phone, delivered tickets and "arranged sitting alongside good-looking girls."

Wenzel eventually "got to be a bus driver—New York to Boston—I worked 13, 15 and 17 hours the first three days. I was supposed to take a training course, but they forgot all about it. The Fourth of July traffic was terrific. At New Haven began the traffic jam. I pulled off the regular route and took the passengers joy riding down the back roads of New England. This got me my nickname, 'Tanglefoot.' It means you don't have sense enough to lift your foot off the accelerator." He concludes, "It was the best job I ever had. I often thought I should have kept it."

"THEY CALLED ME THE 120-POUND WONDER FROM UC"

WITH NO JOBS TO CHOOSE FROM during the Depression, John Sherman, '38 mechanical engineering grad, worked his first co-op in the federal Civilian Conservation Corps in West Virginia. He built roads, hoisted telephone poles and even put down a few forest fires. "We not only fought forest fires, but rattlesnakes, too," he recalls.

"We killed about a dozen rattlesnakes as we erected Burning Rock Fire Tower, and we'd fight fires all night long throughout the mountains. There were so many because the moonshiners regularly started fires to camouflage the smoke that gave away the position of their stills. They (the moonshiners) didn't want the federal agents to spot the telltale signal smoke of their stills. Of course, the moonshiners had the initiative and were always just one step ahead of us all the time. We always said what we'd do if we caught them because they were making so much work for us. It was all pick-and-shovel work to stop those fires, building fire breaks and then starting back fires. You'd work all night, into the day, no sleep, filthy dirty, hot, too. We didn't have any machinery, no bulldozers, no cranes."

Sherman, now 90, adds that the CCC camps brought young men of every economic background together, and some of the fellows were quite tough, so much so that the UC co-op students made it a point to "work and play well with the others." He states, "I learned to get along with all sorts of people. That's the best thing I ever got from co-op. There was only one UC co-op student in our camp who didn't last long. He was feisty and tried to throw his weight around with some of these fellows. They were a pretty rough, tough bunch, and these guys weren't going to take that."

What with hard work and food that came in fits and starts, Sherman says he earned the nickname the "120-pound wonder of UC."

"Every month a trailer of food came with pork chops, raw onions, prunes, apples, hominy, beans. We ate good early in the month and were down to nothing but beans, beans, beans by the end of it," he laughs. It didn't help that the crew did "dumb things" at first, like leaving large milk urns of stew out in the sun, causing dysentery for the whole bunch. "We learned and stopped doing that pretty quick," he recollects.

Brains, Not Brawn
UC co-op students were part of the very first Civilian Construction Corps contingent at Camp Wyoming in West Virginia. Squad 11 was an all co-op contingent. First row, from left to right, are Carroll McBeth, (Martin or Robert) Miller and John Sherman. Standing, from left, are Richard Krauss, Leo Beckett, Walter Clark, Charles Heckel, William Roberts and Gerhard Lessman. For painfully obvious reasons, they called themselves "The Bone Trust."

Certificate of Discharge from Civilian Conservation Corps

JOHN SHERMAN, '38, REMEMBERS that after his time in the CCC had expired, no co-op job could be found for him. So, he went up to Michigan to camp. In the meantime, the local gas and electric company called UC Professor Ralph Van Wye, pictured at right, with an opening for a co-op student. So began Van Wye's odyssey to find Sherman.

Sherman says, "Professor Van Wye visited our German landlords, but they didn't know where we were exactly. They said my mother had a friend named Rowena down the street. Then Professor Van Wye visited Rowena, and she said she didn't know where we were but that I had a friend named St. Clair in town.

Ralph Van Wye

"Professor Van Wye proceeded to call every St. Clair in the phone book till he found my friend. My friend told him that we were up at Green Lake in Michgan. So then he called the post office at Bendon, Mich., where our mail came to, and told the postman to go down to our cottage and find me.

"The next thing I know, the postman came to our cottage and told me, 'Be at the post office in Bendon tomorrow at noon. You're going to receive a long-distance call.' So, I did it, and when Professor Van Wye gets me on the phone, he's yelling, 'Where the hell have you been?! Do you want a co-op job or not?!' I said, 'Heck yes!' and returned to Cincinnati right away."

John Sherman's "home away from home" on his first co-op—the federal Civilian Conservation Corps camp in West Virginia.

Buying in:
Co-op's "change"-ing times

CO-OP

27½ ¢ per

> *"One can buy anything with money except morality and citizens."*
>
> —*Jean-Jacques Rousseau, 1712–1778*
> *Swiss-born French philosopher*

Buying in:
Co-op's "change"-ing times

1906

Co-op students earn 8 to 10 cents an hour.

1921

Civil engineering student Jack Krausser worked on a dam-construction project in Lockport, Ohio: "We worked 72 hours a week, six 12-hour days. We made 35 cents an hour, which was nice income for someone who couldn't go anywhere anyway while we were on the job."

1931

Student Robert Watkins recalls that his senior year co-op in 1931 paid $25 a week. As wages continued to fall during the Depression, it took him three years and 12 jobs to climb back to that $25-a-week high-water mark.

1941

William Geisler started as a co-op student earning 45 cents an hour at Crosley Corp., but the pay rose rapidly as World War II heightened demand for workers. Soon, Geisler was making more than his co-op advisor, but the rationing enforced by 1942 meant there were fewer goods to buy.

1957

Accounting co-op student Sam Sovilla started on his first co-op with Mercantile Stores at a salary of $1 an hour.

1978

A co-op student in design, architecture and art earned about $600 per month (about $30 a workday); in business, about $650 per month; and in engineering, more than $700 per month.

1986

Nationally, the average co-op student earned $6.49 an hour, more than 60 times what their original counterparts did in 1906.

2006

The average hourly wage of a co-op is now about $13, more than a hundredfold increase in the 100 years since 1906.

Add it all up …

And UC's 4,000 co-op students are each earning between $1,700 and $2,500 per month—a collective $30 million per year.

UC's co-op students begin alternating work and school on a seven-week basis.

◄————————— 1932 ————————————————————————— 1933 ———————————————————————— 1934 —————————►

Amelia Earhart becomes the first woman to fly nonstop across the U.S.

A five-day workweek is established for General Motors employees.

As a job-creation program, the Civilian Conservation Corps is signed into law, eventually employing 1,730,000 young men in camps all over the country.

Co-op's contributions:
Key to Cincinnati history

Above is the canal that is now Central Parkway. You can see Mt. Adams in the background. Right is a photo of the newly completed Central Parkway taken in 1928.

> *"I change myself, I change the world."*
>
> —*Gloria Anzaldua, 1942–2004*
> *American scholar, writer and cultural theorist*

Co-op's contributions:
Key to Cincinnati history

Co-op has served as a quiet cornerstone in forming the city's growth since 1906. But more than that, the program has helped lay a foundation for national institutions and essential progress. For instance, co-op students helped ready the first exhibits at Chicago's Museum of Science and Industry and helped build Lookout Mountain National Park in Georgia. One-time civil engineering co-op student Robert Curtis, '39, wrote, "My first co-op was as a member of the surveying crew laying out the first, and still only, road through the Great Smokey Mountains from Gatlinburg, Tenn., to Cherokee, N.C."

Closer to home, yesterday and today, co-op's imprint is all over the city of Cincinnati. Most recently, co-op grads helped build the Greater Cincinnati International Airport and the internationally recognized Contemporary Arts Center. But look back further and the visible markers of co-op's handiwork rise up from almost a century ago. Co-op students helped form the outlines of modern-day Cincinnati by helping to:

- Fill in the canal that became Central Parkway
- Build the city's nascent subway
- Lay out the communities of Mariemont and Greenhills
- Build Union Terminal and the Western Hills Viaduct
- Build the Carew Tower
- Bail out the city during the great flood of 1937

Central Parkway

In 1907, George Kessler, a Kansas City landscape architect, developed the "Kessler Plan," calling for a wide road along the route of the Miami-Erie Canal, which had once provided cheap, reliable transportation of goods and passengers before the advent of railroad and auto. The canal, long little more than an enticement to little boys, mosquitoes and trash, was filled in to pave the way for Kessler's vision for a grand boulevard 150 feet wide with a central green space. In 1920, work to drain the canal began, and UC co-op students helped in the work. Finally, on Oct. 1, 1928, water gave way to the wheel when Central Parkway opened for traffic. The city celebrated as Mayor Murray Seasongood closed City Hall, adjourned the courts and cancelled mail delivery.

Cincinnati News Record
U.C. MOURNS PASSING OF DEAN SCHNEIDER

Dean Herman Schneider dies.

←————— 1936 ————————————————— 1937 ————————————————— 1939 —————→

The Girl Scouts negotiate a contract with a commercial baker for cookie sales.

The first U.S. fitness club opens in California, pioneering such exercises as the jumping jack.

The newly completed marvel, the Golden Gate Bridge, connecting San Francisco with Marin County opens as 200,000 pedestrians cross the "engineering impossibility." The landmark structure incorporates brick from UC's old McMicken Hall, deliberately placed in his crowning achievement by the bridge's designer and builder, UC alum Joseph Strauss.

Cincinnati Subway

UC co-op students helped build Cincinnati's fledgling subway system consisting of a few miles of above-ground track, two miles of tunnel and an intact platform under the intersection of Race Street and Central Parkway. Just before America's entry into the First World War in 1917, local voters approved the project, which was supposed to have run from downtown north to St. Bernard and then east to Norwood and Oakley. They even set the fare price: 5 cents. The project was eventually buried by the automobile and rising post-War World I construction costs. Work on the partially completed project came to a dead stop in 1926.

Above: Subway tubes were placed in less than half of the originally planned 16-mile line. Inset: West steps of Race Street Station, shot in March 1922.

Mariemont

About 20 UC students worked to survey and serve as draftsmen in building the local community of Mariemont, a model town to the east of the city's core built to resemble an old English village. The project, funded by local philanthropist Mary Emery, broke ground in 1923 as a "national exemplar of town planning." Emery's goal was to provide laborers with a self-contained community of homes, apartments, parks, garden plots, stores, playgrounds, churches, schools and recreation—including a tennis court and nine-hole golf course—near to factories and employment centers.

Greenhills

During the Depression, Roy Thurston, '34 civil engineering grad, dug ditches for the local utility company, helped build

UC co-op students run grade stakes for a Mariemont street. The building in the background is the field headquarters for the engineering staff.

the Carew Tower, did survey work in Kentucky and served as a junior engineer for the area's park board. In 1935, he became chief of the topographic survey party for the Greenhills housing project, built by the federal government in the 1930s as one of only three such green-space experiments—the others being Greendale, Wis., and Greenbelt, Md. Completed in 1938, the construction of Greenhills provided work for 2,500 unemployed men. According to David Moore, municipal manager of the Village of Greenhills in Cincinnati, 15 such communities were originally planned but funds ran short.

Courtesy of the Village of Greenhills

The Village of Greenhills under construction.

The half-dome over the Union Terminal rotunda is 107 feet high, and the project as a whole was built in the art deco style new to the 1920s, featuring strong geometric designs.

Union Terminal and Western Hills Viaduct

"I got so that I could climb around structural steel like Tarzan of the Apes," claims William Wenzel, '34 civil engineering grad, who co-opped his last two years in school helping to complete Cincinnati's historic Union Terminal, an exemplar of art deco style. He adds that the local press of the time said it was "the most expensive railroad terminal ever built." Likely so, as local train companies raised $41 million toward its construction just before the Great Depression derailed the economy in the fall of 1929.

Union Terminal was the last major rail terminal ever built in the United States, and Wenzel recollects, "It was a big job—filling in the Mill Creek Valley over an area half a mile wide and three miles long, getting the dirt by completely eliminating a big hill in the west side of the valley, shuffling railroad track and city streets, rebuilding bridges. I worked on a survey party as rodman, chainman and, ultimately, transitman." (In railroad work, a transitman is actually chief of the group.)

Union Terminal when it was first completed in 1933.

Co-op students also helped to build the Western Hills Viaduct.

Wenzel earned $135 a month as a field engineer on the Union Terminal project while other co-op students did everything from pick-and-shovel work to pouring footings. Albert Lathrop, '32, wrote that his job was to make sure the rounded, ten-inch pipe footings upon which the terminal would rest were driven far into solid ground, as deep as 80 feet, before being filled with concrete. His work hours were 6 a.m.–2 p.m. Then Lathrop morphed into a nightclub musician—literally playing for nothing but his supper—from 10 p.m. to midnight.

Carew Tower

UC co-op students helped with construction of this art deco gem. The building project began in September 1929, one month before the stock-market crash that sunk the country into the Great Depression. The tower was supposed to have been the first of three such art deco towers in the city; however, plans for the other two were dropped during the Depression. Of note: As originally built, the tower had men's restrooms on every floor, but women's restrooms only every five floors because there were so few women working in offices when construction began.

Main Street in downtown Cincinnati, January 1937

Courtesy of the Cincinnati Historical Society

Carew Tower

Drowning in work: The 1937 flood

The New York Times called it a "super-flood," and though UC's perch atop the hills of Burnet Woods spared it from the 1937 floodwaters, the university was forced to close on Jan. 21, right in the middle of exams that day. Students from Kentucky fled from their examination classrooms to make it home before the entrances to the Suspension Bridge sank under the Ohio River that afternoon. Soon enough, dislodged trees and uprooted houses were floating down the river, and before the floodwaters receded in early February, Cincinnatians resigned themselves to brushing their teeth with Coca-Cola.

How bad did things get? Hundreds died and hundreds of thousands were made homeless by the rising tide of misery as the Ohio and Mississippi rivers swelled to record levels after heavy rains and melting snow from the mountains bordering the Ohio Valley combined in a bitter brew. Fifty thousand Cincinnatians had to flee their homes as 60 billion tons of water assailed the Ohio Valley in the space of 25 days, and the Ohio River reared to a nearly unimaginable 80 feet. Privation, as well as typhoid and other diseases, threatened to carry off new victims along the creeping 1,800-mile corridor of bloated yellow water and backed-up sewers that stretched from Ohio to Arkansas.

UC President Emeritus Henry Winkler stated that while the city was flooded, "we certainly weren't flooded with too many people for the work." Thus, UC co-op students were mobilized to provide guard and fire protection at Music Hall, build sandbag bridges and levees, help aid agencies and distribute provisions throughout the city, in addition to transforming the university into a city communications hub.

Electrical engineering co-op students in the university's amateur radio club—born of Herman Schneider's mandated hobby hour—worked atop Swift Hall to operate the campus amateur radio station, 8CAU. Working around the clock,

Cincinnati *Times Star* with UC students on the front page

eating and sleeping in shifts at Professor William Osterbrock's house for two weeks straight, the students were Cincinnati's communication lifeline, the only means the city had to broadcast information during the worst stages of the flood.

The students maintained contact with other communities when city phone lines failed, and they served as a vital link within the city as well. The co-op students not only let worried relatives from afar know that their Cincinnati friends and family were safe but also notified the Red Cross of marooned individuals and saw to it that the Red Cross sent badly needed inoculation serums. The students also related upriver weather and flood conditions to commercial radio stations. The Federal Radio Commission recognized the students' important role, giving them new call letters—W8YX—and granting them the authority to order interfering amateur radio operators off the air.

Professor William Osterbrock

Co-op's really big Band of Brothers
(and sisters)

HITTING HOME!

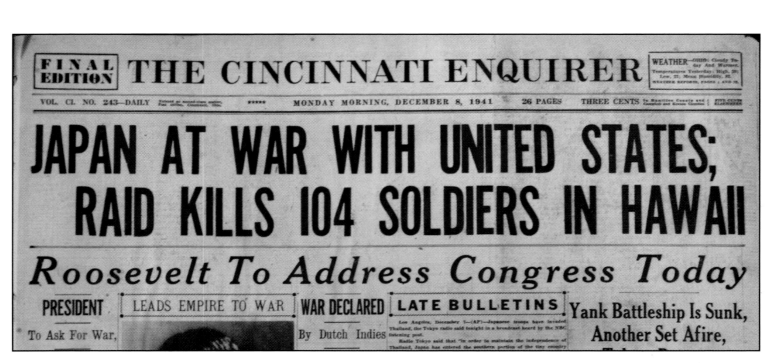

"The purpose of all war is peace."

—*St. Augustine, 354–430*
Christian bishop in Roman North Africa

Co-op's really big Band of Brothers
(and sisters)

The seasons never seemed to change on campus during World War II. Whether springtime or winter, the predominant UC color was olive drab.

But while the seasons didn't seem to change, everything else did. The war's advance on campus scrambled traditional hierarchies. Academic rank was forgotten as McMicken Hall was emptied to provide dormitory space for soldier-students of the 1555th Army Specialized Training Corps. Steel cots replaced desks as professors moved themselves and their libraries from their accustomed quarters to almost anywhere else. Eight fraternity houses were leased for Army use while barracks went up to provide living, dining and classroom space.

Co-op, which had buoyed so many students during the Depression, now ran submerged during the war years—though never officially suspended—as education sprinted rapid-fire to keep step with the march of war. The engineering seniors of 1942 and '43 graduated early. What would have been the engineering class of 1944 became the class of 1943½, graduating in October '43 rather than June '44. In early '43, local high school juniors and seniors skipped their last months or year of high school and came directly to UC as freshmen. One of those, Howard

Marching to class before marching off to save the world
It may seem that campus changed overnight after the Dec. 7, 1941, attack on Pearl Harbor. Not quite so. In anticipation of war, the Reserve Officer Training Corps (ROTC) enrollment in 1940 doubled from what it had been the previous year. With enlistments, enrollment naturally dropped, but national efforts like the Army Specialized Training Program sent enlisted personnel back to campus to study languages, engineering and the physical sciences.

The 1555th Unit began at UC in 1943 and trained more than 2,000 soldiers. On March 10, 1944, the 1555th, pictured above, marched in a farewell parade in front of McMicken Hall.

One-time UC co-op Richard White, then of Hyde Park, is imprisoned in Stalag Luft III in Sagan, Germany, after being shot down in his B-17. The escape activities of that camp are later dramatized in the movie The Great Escape. White's role? "At first, my escape role was that of a 'stooge'... to warn my fellow prisoners when Nazi guards approached. Later, I was promoted to 'penguin'... to help get rid of the sand excavated by others who were digging escape tunnels. As a penguin, I worked in all three escape tunnels, known as 'Tom,' 'Dick' and 'Harry.'"

Due to World War II, almost half of the U.S. institutions with co-op suspend their programs.

←———— 1941 ———————————— 1942 ———————————— 1943 ————→

Japan launches a surprise attack on the U.S. naval base at Pearl Harbor, home of the U.S. Pacific Fleet, forcing America's entry into World War II.

The U.S. government launches its Salvage for Victory campaign to collect tin, rubber, scrap iron, rags and paper for the war effort.

A few months before the U.S. entry into World War II, a segment of the student body had protested against intervention. Now, such divisions were forgotten as students scavenged scrap metal alongside the area's roadsides, participated in research efforts related to the war, entered accelerated training programs, took part in campus prayer services and, of course, enlisted. One research project even required the firing of a simulated rocket, which took place indoors, in a Chemistry Building lab lined with sandbags.

UC co-op student in a lab during World War II. Above him, the placard reads "Remember Pearl Harbor, 24 Hours a Day, 7 Days a Week."

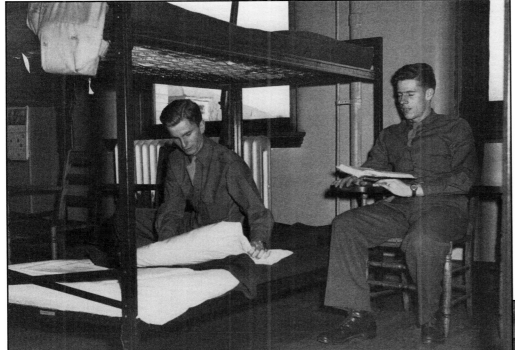

Room 11 in McMicken Hall, once a classroom, was enlisted for use as living space. Making the bed at left is Pvt. John Brown of Saginaw, Mich. Studying at right is Pvt. Charles Leslie of Ashland, Kan.

Niehaus, recalls, "I enrolled at UC in January 1943 in the accelerated engineering program before completing the last half-year of high school. By September, after attending classes all summer, our freshman year was completed."

George Kral, '43 civil engineering grad, who lived in the temporary barracks built in Nippert Stadium and later in Memorial Hall, was among those who graduated early—April 1943 instead of June. "We lost our last co-op and speeded up the course work. What would have been the class of 1944 graduated in the fall of 1943. In later years, they (the class of '44) wound up hanging around with us real '43 guys, but we never really accepted them," jokes Kral.

UC co-ops witness the war's eve and the war's end

Former UC co-op students saw the war begin, and they also helped to end it. Craig Edwards, mechanical engineering class of '37, made a bit of co-op history when he became the first co-op student employed by Bendix Aviation Corporation in South Bend, Ind.

He saw much more of history when he developed an

"airbox" used for testing airplane carburetors, and Bendix sent him to aviation plants in Western Europe in 1939. That's how Edwards happened to be in Paris in May 1940 as the Germans advanced on the city. Planning his getaway, Edwards bought a used car and started hoarding gasoline a little at a time. Fourteen hours before Adolf Hitler's occupation troops took over the city, he fled toward the southern port of Marseilles. Unable to get aboard American export ships there, he continued his 15-day trek, this time heading for Lisbon, Portugal. There, Edwards managed to find a U.S. freighter willing to carry him on the 11-day sea journey to New York City.

Recalling those days, he later wrote how refugees jammed the roads, walking and traveling "in every means of conveyance, and progress was difficult." The only way Americans could imagine it is to picture Chicago's millions heading toward South Bend, Ind.—all on one road.

While Edwards saw the war begin in Europe, another former co-op student helped to end it in the Pacific. It was

1940 co-op grad Jack Binns Sr. who furthered the training efforts for Paul Tibbets (also a UC alum), pilot of the August 1945 ending-the-war mission over Hiroshima, Japan, wherein the use of the atom bomb secured an immediate peace without an invasion of the Japanese homeland.

A lieutenant in the Navy, Binns served as a field engineer in and around the Great Lakes. Basically, he made sure that training cockpits got out of the labs and to the pilots who needed them, a job he was given because of co-op and industry experience. He says, "At Cincinnati Milling Machine, I learned to run all the machine tools during co-op. I made machine patterns in the pattern shop. Co-op gave me familiarity with tools, operations and the industry. So, when I was hired there after graduation, I knew all the work and became an expediter on the assembly line."

At the height of World War II, Binns took on the same job for the military—expediter. He recollects, "We'd have pilot-training devices, training cockpits that worked just like

Flag raising on UC Co-op Day, 1942. Left to right are co-op students Robert Tour, chemical engineering '42; Dick Tullis, business '47; and Wilburn Pean, mechanical engineering '42.

Co-op's Jack Binns Sr. helped bring the war to a close by getting pilots into their training cockpits. His last assignment for the military was to ship the training cockpit for the *Enola Gay* and its ending-the-war mission.

Co-op's really big Band of Brothers (and sisters)   85

Taken by a Cincinnati photographer, the above photo shows crowds gathering as World War II ended in 1945.

Paul Tibbets in the *Enola Gay*.

the real ones where you could mimic the wind, rain and other things to see what would happen to a bomb load and where it would fall under certain weather and atmospheric conditions. I was working 24 hours a day to get these things out of the labs and to the pilots. Basically, they'd be sitting in some lab somewhere, ready to go, and still not be shipped, and I'd be the expediter.

"I remember one such case. The device was supposed to ship the day before. It was still on a slab. A Naval inspector had the specs in front of him, saying that the paint was wrong; it didn't meet specs. I was just a lieutenant, but I took the specs out of his hand, changed the specs so they read that the cockpit should be whatever color it already was. 'Now it meets specs,' I said.

"He replied, 'Either you or I are going to be out of here tomorrow.' The next day, I showed up, and he was gone."

The last training cockpit that Binns worked to get out the door and on its way was for the Paul Tibbets' plane, the *Enola Gay*. "Then," says Binns, "the war was over."

A Cincinnati Co-op
Killed in Action

ONE-TIME CINCINNATI CO-OP LT. Wesley Nelson, a navigator on a B-29 bomber, was killed in Italy. His commanding officer sent the following letter to Nelson's wife, Beth: "They lost an engine while taking off. ... There was nothing left to do then but set the plane down in the field ahead. Wes went to the nose and tried to salvo the bomb load before they hit. Beth, it was a heroic thing for him to do and something you can always be proud of. ... The following day, April 11th, George Matsen and I attended the funeral. ... Wes was laid to rest in a military cemetery in southern Italy. ... Wes died a hero—attempting to save his crew. ... He loved you very much, of that we are all certain."

By the navigator of his crew

Our crew had remained together since leaving the states. However, many times one or more of us would fly on other crews. I had been on D. S. and returned the evening of April 8th to find we were all flying the next two days but I was scheduled on another crew. The four of us had received packages and spent the evening in a holiday mood.

The mission went off fine the next day and that added to our spirits. We spent the evening of the 9th in a very gay mood. We had plenty of eats, a good "Bull Session" and all in all, plenty of fun.

The accident happened during "take off" the next morning. Just what did happen is not entirely clear, but here is as much as I can give you now. They lost an engine while taking off. Doug got the machine engine started again and was attempting to come back into the field when he lost two more engines. There was nothing left to do then but set the plane down in the field ahead. Wes went to the nose and tried to salvo the bomb load before they hit. Beth, it was a heroic thing for him to do and something you can always be proud of. Doug did a beautiful job in beinging the plane in and had it not been for his ability and efforts, no one would have lived.

The following day, April 11th, George Matsen and I attended the funeral services. Wes was laid to rest in a military cemetery in southern Italy, with full military honors. The following day Whit passed on and I attended his services.

Beth, there is little I can say to make things easier for you, but these things I know to be true. Wes died a hero -- attempting to save his crew. His death was instant. He loved you very much, of that we were all certain.

Where there's a war, there's a way: Women storm the workforce

THE TRADITIONAL BATTLE BETWEEN the sexes was anything but uniform in those war years. One male GI ran as a candidate for UC freshman queen in 1943 and won the election, and overall women found themselves summarily promoted. As a war-emergency measure, two-year certificate programs began on the co-op basis in the College of Engineering and Commerce. And for the first time ever, women were admitted into *all* engineering courses and programs.

While saving bacon grease to make explosives and planting victory gardens, women by the millions—six million, to be exact—responded to the call as Red Cross volunteers, pilots and even spies. But most filled the ranks as laborers on the assembly line, soldiering on in the pitched industrial battle between Allies and Axis. Co-op employers balked at first, but eventually began hiring women in greater numbers for production positions. For instance, in 1943, the Frigidaire Co. of Dayton employed its first UC woman co-op as a test case. By October 1944, a total of eight women co-op students were with the company, then producing aircraft propellers and machine guns in lieu of refrigerators.

And co-op made the difference in preparing UC women students to competently take on *manufacturing* jobs. So recalls 1942 business graduate

Florence Endebrock Schroeder. At the time of her graduation, Schroeder wrote in a campus publication, "The co-op [students] have been able to adapt themselves to war industries more easily and have been better trained to begin

immediate production due to their cooperative work." She then went on to prove her point by going to work, first for Carnegie-Illinois Steel Corp. in Pittsburgh and then for Wright Aeronautical Corp., one of the nation's largest World War II employers (and a co-op employer),

manufacturer of tens of thousands of aircraft engines.

Looking back, Schroeder says, "The war absolutely helped women students. Out-of-town corporations came to recruit us girls. We'd previously been prepared to be secretaries, but I was hired out of school for $125 a month to do far more. I was tracking the company's financial operations, keeping stats, making financial forecasts, projecting sales and measuring cash flow." She laughs, "We were the ones basically telling the company [Carnegie-Illinois Steel] when they needed to go to the bank to borrow more money."

By the end of the war, Schroeder recalls that her salary had rocketed to $350 a month. She'd also learned to play golf—courtesy of her employers, who wanted the women to quickly get into the swing of traditional corporate structures. In the process, she'd gone further than she or her family had ever thought possible: "My father was not a blue-collar worker—he was black collar, a worker in a foundry. When I started college, he'd been out of work for six years. My family had nothing. Co-op, UC and—truth be told—the war, as horrendous as it was, were godsends for me. I don't know what I would have done otherwise."

Women in the war
WE CAN'T WIN WITHOUT THEM

Courtesy of the Cincinnati Historical Society

Florence Endebrock Schroeder is on the catwalk, at far left, in a UC industrial chemistry lab. On the catwalk with her are Mary Andrew and George Pow. At bottom, from left, are Ralph Schneider and Wallace Allen. The photo was taken in preparation for the March 28, 1942, Co-op Day celebrations.

War and Circumstance

Florence Endebrock Schroeder and classmates graduated a little early that wartime spring: April 10, 1942. She recalls, "We graduated right after Pearl Harbor. The boys wore their ROTC uniforms under their caps and gowns and left immediately for the service from the commencement ceremonies. By April 20, I was on the job in Pittsburgh for a subsidiary of U.S. Steel, not as a secretary but as a statistical accountant. Before the war, the women had been secretaries, but during the war, the employers hired us for men's positions. They even gave us girls golf lessons so we could fit in."

Day-off duties

Already working in Pittsburgh by October 1942 when this photo was shot, former UC co-op student Florence Endebrock Schroeder recalls that "as something to do on her day off," she served coffee and doughnuts from a Salvation Army Mobile Canteen to servicemen at Pennsylvania Station.

Experience of every stripe

REGISTRATION CERTIFICATE

This is to certify that in accordance with the
Selective Service Proclamation of the President of the United States

Selig *Hoff* *Isaacs*
(First name) (Middle name) (Last name)

2805 Dugby Cincinnati O.
(No. and street or R. F. D. No.; city or town, county and State)

has been duly registered this *16* day of *Oct* , 19 *40*

Elsie Fischer
(Signature of registrar)

Registrar for *N* *12* *Cincinnati O*
(Precinct) (Ward) (City or county) (State)

BE ALERT { Keep in touch with your Local Board.
          Notify Local Board immediately of change of address.
CARRY THIS CARD WITH YOU AT ALL TIMES

D. S. S. Form 2   16—17105

Selig F. Isaacs
(Registrant must sign here)

DESCRIPTION OF REGISTRANT

RACE		HEIGHT (Approx.)	WEIGHT (Approx.)	COMPLEXION	
		5-8	170	Sallow	
White	✓	EYES	HAIR	Light	
		Blue	Blonde	Ruddy	✓
Negro		Gray	Red	Dark	
Oriental		Hazel	Brown ✓	Freckled	
		Brown ✓	Black	Light brown	
Indian		Black	Gray	Dark brown	
			Bald	Black	
Filipino					

Other obvious physical characteristics that will aid in identification

Draft card carried by UC co-op student Ted Isaacs in 1940

> *"Victory is a thing of the will."*
>
> —*Ferdinand Foch, 1851–1929*
> *French Marshall*

Experience of every stripe

By 1942, Warren Badger, a '41 co-op grad barely into his 20s, found himself in Liberia, in charge of a factory running 24 hours a day to produce latex rubber for the U.S. war effort.

Charles Harris, '33 mechanical engineering co-op grad, supervised General Motors' huge Moraine plant and was one of a team of three to coordinate changing the facilities over from building Frigidaires to turning out 5,000 complete propeller units each month for use by Allied fighters and bombers. At the war's close, he did the same job but in reverse.

Thomas Hold, '27 civil engineering grad, commanded the 343rd Engineer Regiment's First Battalion, which included 13 other former UC engineering co-op students, in the construction of the Capua Bridge over Italy's Volturno River in 1943. Their combined expertise helped create the longest military bridge in history at that time. The almost-400-foot structure, made from materials at hand, was completed under fire in a record 20 days. It was the only bridge to survive on the river, which frequently reached flood stage. More than one million vehicles of every type passed over the bridge in the six months following its construction.

Army recruit Eugene Roth, '32 mechanical engineering grad, in the Middle East, would have liked to switch postings with Homer Hornung, a fellow co-op grad from the electrical engineering class of

---

┌───┐
│ **EVERYMAN'S PLEDGE**
│
│ AMERICA SHALL WIN THIS WAR!
│
│ Therefore, I will work, I will save, I will sacrifice, I will endure, I will fight–cheerfully, and to my utmost–as if the whole issue of the struggle depended on me alone.
└───┘

First-term enrollment at the College of Engineering stands at 2,073, the largest in the history of the college: 2,044 men, 29 women.

1944

President Franklin Roosevelt signs the GI Bill of Rights authorizing a broad package of benefits, including a college education, for World War II veterans.

1945

World War II ends.

1946

Labor strikes are the worst in U.S. history.

The first African American switchboard operator is hired by Pacific Telephone and Telegraph Company.

Sgt. Robert Scott on Kodiak Island

Sgt. Charles Loudon

Cpl. John Hieronymus

Former Cincinnati co-ops circle the globe in World War II
• Top left, Sgt. Robert Scott on Kodiak Island, Alaska.
• Above, Cpl. John Hieronymus in Iran with his unit's very young interpreter.
•Right, Capt. Louis Luechauer taught chemical warfare and other subjects at Camp Lee, Va., before eventually winding up atop this Egyptian camel.
• Far right, Lt. Chuck McClintock, an Army engineer, was with the first U.S. company to land at Normandy. His job: to blow up enemy installations on the beach. This photo was taken in 1945 when McClintock was in Belgium.
•Top right, Sgt. Charles Loudon served with the 15th American Air Force in Italy as a gunner with a B-24 Liberator squadron. In this photo, he's watching a formation of bombers land after a mission in Germany.

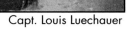

Capt. Louis Luechauer

Lt. Chuck McClintock in Belgium

'38, who spent more than two years in Iceland with the Signal Corps. Roth wrote home, "A little rain would be a welcome exchange for one of our many dust storms," adding that he found sand in his "bunk, eats and hair all the time."

Former co-op student Robert Gossling, civil engineering class of '38, fought in the Pacific's Makin, Saipan and Okinawan invasions, thereby earning a Bronze Star and Purple Heart. What's more, he brought his wife with him. Gossling married an Army nurse in Schofield Barracks, Hawaii, in 1944, and when her field hospital was moved to Saipan in August 1944, they became the only married couple serving together among the U.S. forces there.

Co-op companies make for the front lines: Cincinnati war production

After Pearl Harbor, the following Cincinnati co-op firms literally switched gears and ramped up production, turning the city into a wartime arsenal against Adolf Hitler and the Axis powers.

Company	Peacetime production	Wartime production
Baldwin Piano Company	Pianos	Plane parts
Crosley Corporation	Appliances	Plane parts
General Motors	Cars	Gun mounts
Herschede Hall Clock Company	Clocks	Gun sights

Companies making more of what they made before the war

Allis-Chalmers	Electric motors
American Laundry Machinery	Laundry machines
Cincinnati Milling Machine Company	Machine tools
E. Kahn's Sons Company	Meat products
Emery Industries	Candles and chemicals
Procter & Gamble	Soap and chemicals
R.K. LeBlond Machine Tool Company	Machine tools

New wartime plants and products in Greater Cincinnati

Wright Aeronautical Corporation	Aircraft engines

Courtesy of the Cincinnati Historical Society

POST WAR TO PRESENT:
CHANGE IS THE ONLY CONSTANT

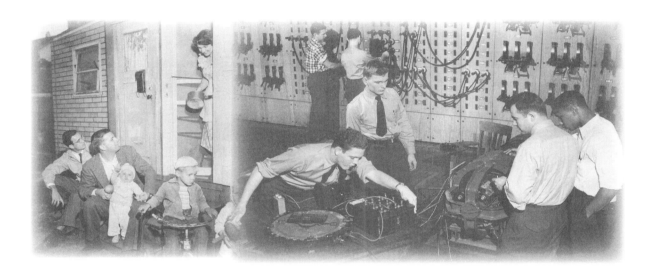

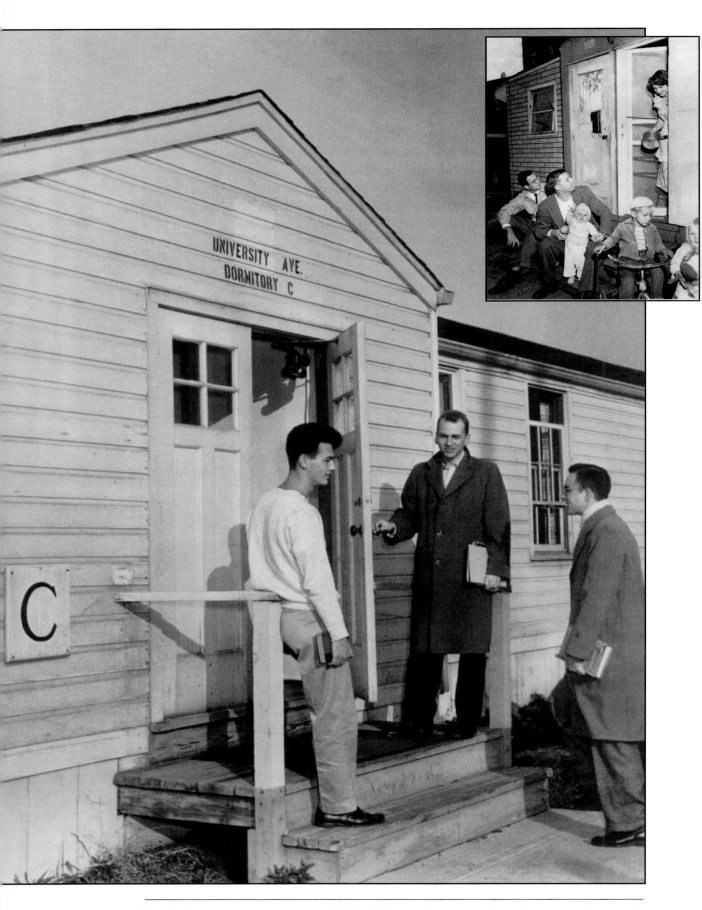

Though the war was over, campus still looked like a military camp. Barracks continued to provide classroom space and, most important, living quarters. Individual household quarters in the barracks were 36 feet long and 8 feet wide, for families as large as five people. There was no room inside Vetsville, as it was called, for such "luxuries" as playpens, oversized chairs or even ovens. So meals were cooked on hot plates, and work, play and socializing took place out of doors for the most part.

> *"I will prepare, and some day, my chance will come."*
>
> —*Abraham Lincoln, 1809–1865*
> *U.S. President*

In the wake of war:
New battle lines are drawn

There was no return to "normal" after World War II. Neither work nor study retreated to the dreary crawl of the Depression years. Rather, campus and co-op pulsed and quickened.

Students flooded into the university, no longer inexperienced youths. Mature men and women of purpose, they came back and burst the seams of campus, striding long-legged and confident into the classroom and workplace. Veterans, mostly men taking advantage of the GI Bill, coaxed the hesitating gears of civilian life—along with their wives and children—within the corseted confines of the 36-by-8-foot barrack space provided to each family.

So by 1947, campus contained nearly 20,000 students (plus relatives), and between 1950–54, eight new buildings were

"I'll start at the bottom."

Once emblematic of co-op, the "start-at-the-bottom" philosophy depicted in this cartoon sketched by a co-op student was a fast-fading reality after World War II.

dedicated on campus, including residence halls. Although enrollment reached record heights, requests for co-op workers still outpaced the supply of students. And because they were in such demand, co-op students began to immediately assume professional roles during their work quarters. Gone were the days when students literally built their careers from the bottom up, first performing menial, manual work before rising to professional positions.

At least those days were gone for *most* co-op students, but not for the handful of African Americans who broke co-op's color barrier on the heels of World War II. They were a small group known as the "Pioneers," coming to UC at a time when racial segregation in the United States was palpably real even as Cincinnati's black population grew by 41 percent in the 1940s and '50s.

Moviemaker Steven Spielberg's father, Arnold M. Spielberg, graduates from the co-op electrical engineering program. Steven's uncle Irvin Spielberg graduated from the aeronautical engineering program in 1941 and went to work at Wright-Patterson Air Force Base, returning to UC on occasion to lecture as an authority on vibration and flutter.

Henry Thomas Brown of Cincinnati's West End becomes the first African American to enroll in UC's co-op program.

1949 ———————— 1950 ———————————— 1952 ————→

PEZ candy is introduced in the U.S. after originating in Austria as a breath mint for cigarette smokers.

The barracks that sprouted all over campus after Pearl Harbor remained until 1957. One was even situated in the middle of Nippert Stadium since football was discontinued during the war as athletes went into the service rather than out for the team. Mechanical engineering student Robert Nolte recollects living in the Nippert barracks: "My first year in Cincinnati, I lived in the economy dormitory located in Nippert Stadium. It was operated for freshman men at a charge of 50 cents a week." George Kral, '43, did the same, living in Nippert's barracks for a year before moving to Memorial Hall. He first chose to live in the barracks because he could do so for "practically nothing," he says. "We were just a bunch of guys in one big room." When the last Vetsville barracks came down in the late 1950s, it signaled a new era and new beginnings.

While co-op had never "officially" been off-limits to blacks, these minority students had been effectively barred from engineering and business programs because of the co-op requirement in these programs. They could not fulfill that requirement since employers would not accept them for co-op positions.

One former co-op coordinator recalled, "To place blacks, you had to canvas the whole area. It was never easy. To place African American women, that was the hardest of all." Former co-op head Sam Sovilla confirms, "You had to try and counteract the resistance to African Americans both in the classroom and in the workplace. We'd send a well-qualified African American junior or senior co-op on an interview with younger, less-qualified white students, hoping the employer would opt to hire the African American."

The first black students in UC's co-op course were Henry Thomas Brown and Clark Beck, who graduated together in 1955. Both remember those years as ones of intense personal struggle.

Before coming to UC, Beck had actually tried to enter Purdue University after first earning a mathematics degree from Virginia Union University. He recalls, "After I got that first degree, I set out to do what I'd wanted to do all along, go to engineering school. I proudly drove to Purdue with my mother and with my transcript in hand. The dean there wouldn't even open the envelope to look at the transcript. He said that I should go into the industrial arts to teach my people how to build houses. He said that my people couldn't be engineers.

"He broke my heart, and I left with tears in my eyes. Mom and I drove straight from there to UC because I'd heard of the co-op program, and I figured it would pay my way after the first year. Even though I arrived unannounced, the dean came out of a meeting to see me. He looked at my transcript and said, 'You can come if you want to, but you'll catch hell.'"

Brown similarly recalls that in those days, all students submitted photos with college applications. After applying to study chemical engineering at UC in 1949, he received a letter asking him to come in for a summertime interview. "I took the letter to the only professional I knew, a lawyer at the YMCA," Brown says. "He read it and said, 'You'll be interviewed to tell you the hardships of engineering, to be told that no black has ever been there before, and they've never had a black graduate.' That's just what happened, too. It was done to discourage me from entering, but at the end of that interview, I just said, 'Thank you. I'll be here in September.'"

Henry Thomas Brown, one of two of the first African American co-op grads, attended this 1955 UC Mardi Gras dance in the Great Hall during his final months at UC. He was among a small handful of minorities in attendance. "Many of the black students didn't feel at ease at the various social functions and, consequently, did not participate in them," he says. "Those of us who did attend had made a special effort to get other black students out but only succeeded with three African American couples going to the affair." There was a payoff though. Henry and his companion, Melinda Wells, were named King and Queen of the dance after they captured a balloon containing the lucky "King and Queen" slip.

Kraut, Kike, Red !

As this campus cartoon and this campus headline attest, humor based on gender and race greeted women, blacks and other minorities who entered co-op as well as other college programs throughout the country.

Because of their cooperative work experiences, however, many co-op students seemed more open than society as a whole. A 1923 co-op grad later wrote that as a freshman, he worked a construction job in which he dug ditches with African American laborers. "I got in the middle of the line and was working my head off when the old, colored man behind me touched me on the shoulder so he could show me how to use a pick and shovel. Though this man could neither read nor write, he used the engineering principles of leverage in performing his duties. Here was a man who was an *expert*. [I learned] no one needs a degree in order to be an expert."

Just as with the very first band of co-ops and the first women in the program, personal determination drove the initial group of African American students within the co-op program. Still, in this instance, determination was a solid rock ramming itself against a high, hard wall. In that time, so reluctant were employers to hire minority students that it was only government installations or those companies with large government contracts that served as available employment sources for blacks in the co-op program.

Brown still remembers that even though his grades were so good that he made the dean's list every quarter and eventually just missed graduating first in his engineering class, UC could not find him an actual engineering co-op. "At first, my coordinator could only find me a laborer's position on the factory floor of Republic Steel up in Cleveland," he states. "I filled in on positions for people while they were on vacation. But, it was money, and I took the co-op." Except for one year's co-op in industry, Brown had to work the remainder of his co-op quarters in campus labs.

Likewise, Beck struggled throughout his UC years even while the American economy boomed after World War II. His first year at the university was grueling. First, no place near campus would rent to him. Beck says, "They were always 'all full.'" At last, he found lodging in Walnut Hills, a single room in a three-story house. No running water. No kitchen. No refrigerator.

Beck adds, "I had absolutely no money and ate nothing but canned meats and canned goods my mother sent me

Registration of late 1950 co-op students and the staff of *The Co-Operative Engineer* are pictured here. Tellingly, the photos include no women and no minority students.

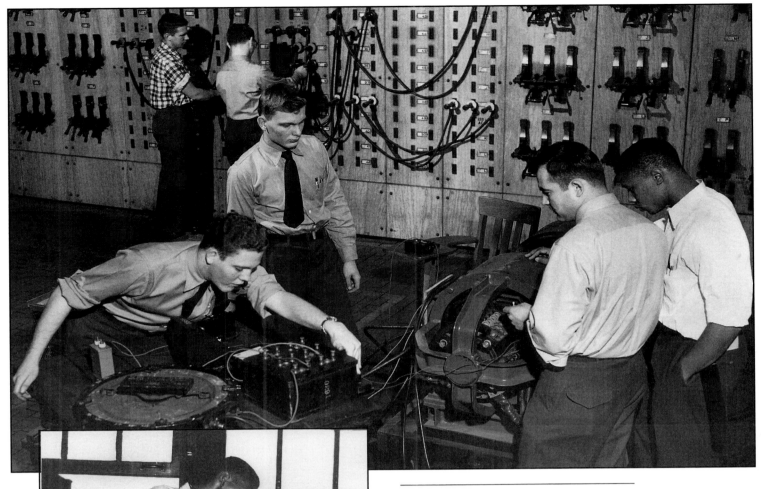

Two members of the Pioneers: Lamar Cox in a lab (above); and Ben Moore Sr., seated in a classroom (at left).

in care packages. I'd eat half a can in the morning, set it on the windowsill outside in the winter cold, and then eat the other half at night. I hated it when the classroom was quiet, and everyone could hear my stomach growl. I hated the quiet because I had to cough so bad or sneeze, because I was so often sick with strep throat, which brought up a green mucous. Those were terrible years. I survived, but barely."

Both of these men—Beck and Brown—state that there were always some co-op students who didn't return to campus from their work assignments, opting to drop out or enter another area of study. Today, Beck laughs, "They were always surprised to see me coming back, but I did. Day by day, I got through. I was determined, and I always remembered a phrase attributed to Abraham Lincoln: 'I will prepare, and some day, my chance will come.'"

COURTING TROUBLE:
THE CO-OP TRAP

BECAUSE OF CO-OP, BASKETBALL legend Oscar Robertson found himself fair game for the National Collegiate Athletic Association.

Robertson began playing for the UC Bearcats varsity team in his sophomore year, 1957–58. That same year, he began co-opping for the Cincinnati Gas & Electric Co.—passing between academic

Langsam quickly countered that co-op was integral to education at UC: First, it was a requirement to graduate from certain programs. Second, students *were* actually enrolled while on co-op, and their work reviews routinely came back to the university for oversight and a co-op grade.

Then the wrangling began. The NCAA took about a year to reach a decision

and work terms just like any other student.

Only Robertson wasn't just any other student. He was arguably the greatest all-around player in basketball history, also standing tall as a barrier breaker. As such, Robertson recalls that he was bull's-eye visible, such that the NCAA—the governing body for college sports—noted his co-op career and almost elbowed him off the court because of it.

In 1958, the NCAA was examining co-op and athletics at colleges around the country, and the organization basically charged that if Robertson was in the workplace rather than the classroom every day, he wasn't a student and, therefore, was ineligible to play the game. Then UC President Walter

that, yes, co-op could be properly characterized as education. But the decision came too late for Robertson.

"I wanted to co-op because of the inspiration provided by my teachers at Crispus Attucks High School," he says. "They prepared you for challenges and really encouraged you to experience life, try different avenues to find out what you wanted to do with your life," Robertson adds. "But I didn't continue with co-op" because of the warning whistles sounded by the NCAA.

"Coach [George] Smith came to me one day and said that I wasn't in the [co-op] program anymore. What could I say? There was nothing to say, so I said, 'OK.'"

Oscar Robertson still scoring points
One-time UC business student Oscar Robertson, perhaps the greatest all-around basketball player in the history of the game, remembers that he loved his stint as a co-op student, "pricing conduit materials with the guys" at Cincinnati Gas & Electric Co. "It was a great experience," he reminisces. "I think every college should have co-op. I grew as a person because of the people I met. I was really quite shy when I came to the university, and co-op helped me to learn to communicate with people. I got to see corporate life as it really is, not what the books say it is." Perhaps because he is so identified with his basketball persona, Robertson might get less credit than he should for his academic and business achievements. While a fully committed athlete and business student, he co-opped for a year and made the dean's list a number of times. Upon his graduation in 1960, he straight away co-captained the U.S. Olympic gold-medal basketball team and went on to a golden basketball career followed by a sure-footed business one, serving as president of Orchem, ORDMS and Orpack-Stone, with interests in banking, real estate and media.

WITH SOLDIERS ON THE FRONT LINES, BLACKS WERE ON THE FIRING LINE

TO UNDERSTAND THE FORMIDABLE resistance that African American students confronted upon entering the co-op program, it may be helpful to look at a stinging incident in local history, an event that occurred just five years before the first blacks became co-op students at UC.

It was during the Second World War when industry's manpower famine produced an appetite so sharp for workers that first women and then African Americans were called upon to serve and feed the hearty manufacturing sector. Still, many refused to swallow the equality of black workers.

Right here in Cincinnati, one of the country's largest World War II employers, the huge Wright Aeronautical Corp. – founded just prior to Pearl Harbor as the largest single-story U.S. industrial factory ever built at that time – employed tens of thousands six days a week. But just as the raging battle to free Europe began on Omaha Beach on D-Day in June 1944, more than 15,000 white workers at Wright flew into a rage that seven black workers were promoted, moved from work in the segregated north plant to its nearly all-white central plant.

The company wanted to transfer a handful of African Americans to operate idle machines in order to speed production. Instead, a four-day strike ensued, with laborers claiming they would not return to work "until the question of Negroes working on mechanical assembly lines was settled."

Said one striker at that time, "The company is trying to shove something down our throats, but we won't take this. The company and the union are unpatriotic trying to force us to work alongside Negro workers." Another said, "I don't want to work next to Negroes, and I don't think the boys coming back will want to work with them."

Because the plant was an important link in the military supply chain, a

Courtesy of the Cincinnati Historical Society

Worker training at Wright Aeronautical Corp.

3000 Walk Out At Wright Plant

"strike force" of Air Force, FBI and Army Intelligence personnel all descended on Cincinnati. While an Air Force colonel encouraged workers to return to the assembly lines as the battle for Fortress Europe began, the FBI and Army investigated whether the walk-out had treasonous elements.

In the end, workers returned under the threat of losing their jobs. The seven blacks maintained their lathe-machine posts, and the factory machines that had stood silent on D-Day revved up again. Though a local newspaper labeled the strike "Cincinnati's shame," the trip-wire attitudes that produced it were much harder to reverse than was the seesaw tide of battle in Europe.

A civil-rights protest march in downtown Cincinnati actually grew from less overt equal-rights protests made even during World War II. During the war, colleges and universities across the country published "No Negroes accepted" in their class bulletins, and one local African American paper editorialized: "We are emphasizing all-out training for defense (yet) ... no Negroes accepted even though they be brilliant scholars with latent possibilities. No Negroes accepted even though we need skilled mechanics. No Negroes accepted if our country has been bombed and our ships sunk faster than we can build them. Regardless of everything... No Negroes Accepted.'"

Firsts, bests and boasts

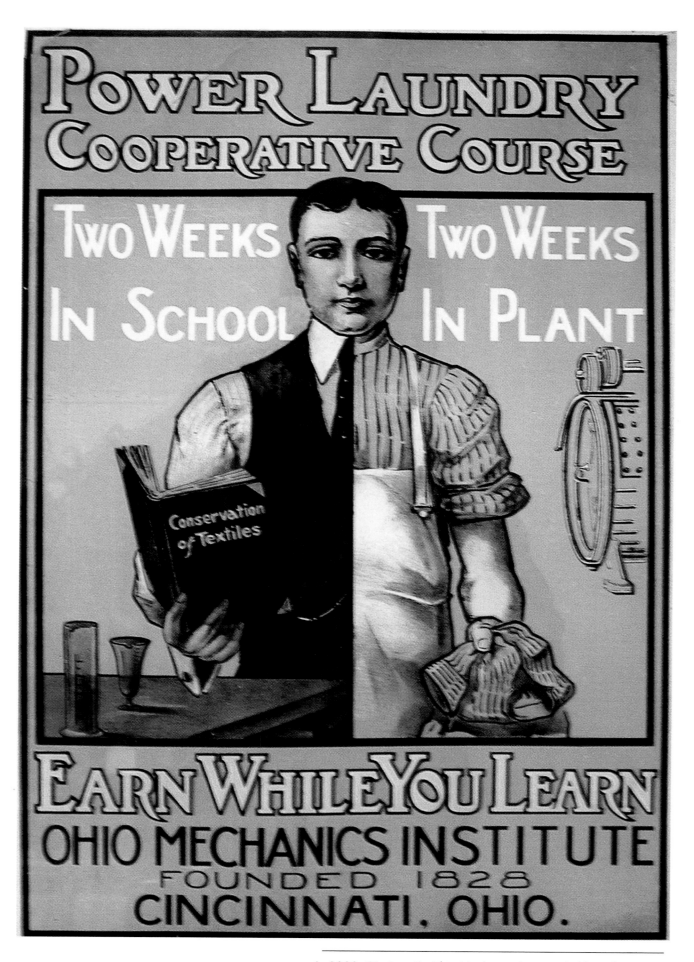

In 1920, Cincinnati's Ohio Mechanics Institute, led by a former UC engineering faculty member, established the first two-year program in co-op—in its power laundry program. The OMI later became part of UC.

> *"The secret of joy in work is contained in one word—excellence. To know how to do something well is to enjoy it."*
>
> —*Pearl S. Buck, 1892–1973*
> *American novelist*

Firsts, bests and boasts

Here's the lowdown on how highly ranked UC co-op is. Time and again, when *U.S. News & World Report* lists the nation's best co-op programs, UC routinely makes the grade among America's top-ten elite.

You might say that we pull rank. After all, UC's undergraduate interior design program is ranked as the nation's best by employers in the field. UC's architecture program is the first among the nation's Top Ten Most Innovative Architecture Programs, and in terms of overall quality, the architecture program is ranked No. 2 in the nation by employers. In addition, employers ranked UC's industrial design program as No. 2 in the nation.

Why? The employers—as well as College of Design, Architecture, Art, and Planning faculty and students themselves—credit co-op as the pivotal booster in those rankings, allowing Midwest UC to beat out privileged eastern rivals like Harvard, Yale, Princeton, Columbia and Cornell.

In fact, UC houses:

• The nation's largest mandatory co-op program, and the largest co-op program at any public institution in the U.S.

• The globe's third-largest co-op program

• The world's largest combined design, architecture and art co-op program

And while UC rightly crows about being the first to found the educational practice, we wear a laurel wreath of other co-op firsts:

1906—Co-op had its worldwide founding at UC.

1915—UC was the first to experiment with the placement of nursing students on co-ops, but a formal, ongoing plan for nurses had to wait till the next century.

1919—UC founded the first co-op program in business.

1920—UC was the first to admit women into co-op.

1920—Cincinnati's Ohio Mechanics Institute (led by a former UC engineering faculty member) established the first two-year program in co-op, power laundry. The OMI later becomes part of UC.

2003—UC founded the first formal co-op program at a College of Nursing.

50th anniversary of co-op
The "Panorama of Progress" exhibit at UC's Field House draws 56,000 visitors and is featured on Radio Free Europe and on the network TV show Today. *Eight members of the original co-op class return to campus: George Binns, Howard Cook, Walston Cragg, Alden Hart, Julian Maas, Ralph McMomas, Richard Paulsen and Oscar Pluedemann.*

◄——— 1954 ——————————————— 1955 ——————————————— 1956 ———►

The Radio Corporation of America begins the manufacture of color TV sets at its Bloomington, Ind., plant. Each set sells for the astronomical sum of $1,000.

Rosa Parks, a 42-year-old seamstress, is arrested in Montgomery, Ala., as she sits on a public bus in a seat reserved for whites. Her actions spark a yearlong boycott of buses by blacks and help launch the U.S. Civil Rights Movement.

Co-op in a tight spot:
Backed into a corner

In the 1960s and '70s, more than one employer figured UC had crossed the line by sending recruiters to the Nippert Stadium press box to interview students. Ralph Murray, a long-time staff member, got up early on snowy mornings to salt down the steel steps leading to the box. He recalls, "One time, a big shot from an accounting firm just stood at the base of the steps telling me, 'I will not even interview. I'm going back to the office.' I coaxed him along by saying, 'You'll be leaving a full schedule of students who will be without interviews.' He finally backtracked after that with, 'Well, I'll go on up.'

> *"No obstacle is insurmountable."*
>
> —*UC alum Joseph Strauss, 1870–1938*
> *Designer and builder of the Golden Gate Bridge, a feat once thought*
> *impossible due to geography, earthquakes, riptides and high winds*

Co-op in a tight spot:
Backed into a corner

Co-op's fortunes were frankly chaotic on the University of Cincinnati campus as the '60s and '70s squeezed out the post-World War II generation. Entering into its full strength, cooperative education indeed relished its coming of age—amply accepted by employers, who practically panted in pursuit of student workers. UC's co-op gleamed, a Cadillac program, having proven itself incomparable in the wider world.

On campus, however, co-op's challenges accumulated. Just as enrollment soared after World War II thanks to the GI Bill, the Baby Boomers sent numbers swelling anew in the late '60s and '70s, resulting in helter-skelter growth.

So while buildings reared up, co-op suffocated for want of

space. Recruiting employers from the era recall interviewing students while contorting themselves into the crannies of the stadium press box or the nooks of halls and labs, spaces that were ugly with a capital "Ugh." One forlorn recruiter piteously requested midwinter "heat in the press box and lights in the biology building," where, by the way, "the smell wasn't too great either," likely from the "dead turtle in the sink."

Sam Sovilla, later head of co-op, admits that UC was guilty as charged. "If ugly and grossly inadequate space had been a felony violation, UC's co-op would have been on death row. I used to have a photo we took of one employer who came on campus to interview. He was actually placed in a tight space in the stadium press box, which

Chemical engineering co-op grad Theodore Brown, '69, states, "I vividly remember working on my senior research project as the anti-Vietnam War demonstrators came through the chemistry building, breaking the glass windows in the laboratory doors."

Neil Armstrong, the first man on the moon, joins UC's College of Engineering to teach co-op students.

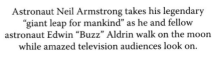

— 1969 —

Astronaut Neil Armstrong takes his legendary "giant leap for mankind" as he and fellow astronaut Edwin "Buzz" Aldrin walk on the moon while amazed television audiences look on.

— 1971 —

— 1972 —

Federal Express is founded by Fred Smith in Memphis, Tenn.

The family drama series *The Waltons* premieres on CBS. The series is based on the life and written works of UC alum Earl Hamner, '48.

also housed a broken commode visible to both the interviewer and students. Other spaces we found for interviews included cloakrooms, hallways or corners over in TUC, where the band would likely be playing right next door during the interview. Frankly, my feelings from that time can be summed up in one word: disgust."

Ron Poole, a '62 finance graduate and former co-op student, was kinder in his judgment of campus when he came back as a recruiter for a local department store. Nevertheless, he also claims, "I did anything I could to avoid UC's facilities even while I made excuses for the school. In the winter, when we recruiters were sent to the press box, both we and the students had to keep our coats on. We couldn't take notes because our hands were so cold, and we couldn't even really face each other and talk. The press-box seating is set on descending risers. Any way you sat, you were craning your head up, down or sideways to try to make eye contact with someone sitting on a different level than you."

Eventually Poole developed his own strategy for interviewing UC students. When the weather was fine, he'd suggest a walk around campus with a potential employee: "We sat around the quadrangle or walked. I would say, 'I haven't been on campus for a while. Let's go and see what's new.' It wasn't true, but the lie was better than the facilities."

Ironically, the grab-bag nature of interviews and facilities during this time of swollen enrollment had something of an upside. "Since company recruiters for co-op and graduating

Ted Brown, '69 chemical engineering grad, states, "The anti-Vietnam protests really came home to me when I was working on my senior project in a chemistry lab. I vividly remember the protestors running through the halls and smashing the glass windows of the professors' office doors. Then they went to the Physics Building and began throwing furniture through the upper-floor windows out onto the lawn. But mostly, the protestors carried signs that said things like, 'Make Love, Not War,' usually at the student union."

students were strewn everywhere at UC, the protestors common to all schools at that time couldn't always find them," Sovilla explains.

Yes, protestors targeted co-op and co-op employers. "For instance," Sovilla continues, "Say Dow Chemical was coming to campus. You knew to put that recruiter in an out-of-the-way, narrow hallway where Vietnam War protestors—who, of course, wanted media attention—couldn't find him or where, at least, TV cameras couldn't fit if they did find him. Protestors would fill the interviewing schedules, never show up for interviews, but then, other students would have missed the chance to interview. We'd have meetings at 7 a.m. to plan how employers could recruit and avoid protests."

Sovilla's long-time colleague Ralph Murray recollects arriving to work one morning at about 8:15 a.m. to find 12 protestors lying in front of his office door. "I said, 'You'll have to move. I have to go to work,'" he explains. "I tried to talk to them like I was their father." No dice. Murray later called the UC police so that he could eventually wedge himself into his office.

He insists, however, that the campus protestors weren't co-op students, and he's likely right. The average co-op student just wasn't of the protesting stripe. "How could we

be?" wondered Ted Brown, a '69 chemical engineering grad. "We weren't in the mainstream because we'd spend 10 weeks on campus in classes but then 13 weeks away working. It was very hard for us to really be in on the ebb and flow of campus. And none of our engineering professors even spoke about the Vietnam War."

Serendipitously, both co-op's battle for adequate designated space on campus and protests against the Vietnam War came to a close around the same time. "The beginning of the end of our 'space wars' began in January 1970 when I walked into our office in Baldwin Hall to find an entire wall just plain gone," states Sovilla. "There was nothing but clear plastic between us and the frigid outdoors."

It seems that some sort of remodeling was on the books, but no one bothered to mention it to the office users. "Recruiting was going to start in a few days," Sovilla adds. "We had no rooms. I was so mad!"

Mad enough that he and other staff staged their own protest. Sovilla and his colleagues simply cancelled all recruiting on campus. Employers howled, loud enough to be heard in then UC President Walter Langsam's office. So in fall 1972, co-op had a new home—*with* interviewing space—in Old Chemistry, where it settled for a peaceful 32 years.

Today's 24-karat co-ops

UC co-op student Kerrie Wallace working at Turner Construction.

Today's 24-karat co-ops

Co-op and the experience it provides land students in some of the most unlikely spots: Underwater helping NASA to train astronauts; in Switzerland helping an oil-spewing plane to land; with the Nuclear Regulatory Commission during the Three Mile Island investigation; helping to design better luge equipment for U.S. Olympic teams; and on the Disney Productions design team, creating an amusement park in Tokyo.

Co-op's testings and trials are as challenging for students today as they were for the program's pioneers in 1906. Indeed, contemporary co-op students are pioneers in their own right, as evidenced by the following sample of achievements.

In the middle of a war

Without leaving Ohio, 1990 aerospace co-op student Damian Olivieri found himself in the middle of a war, the Persian Gulf War that began with Iraq's invasion of Kuwait in August 1990. His co-op work ranged from vulnerability tests of the "Warthog" A-10 aircraft to accelerated production of fuses for the "Hellfire" anti-tank missiles. His analysis of foreign military aircraft was so important that Olivieri found himself on the phone talking to military personnel on the ground in Europe and the Middle East. "I had calls from all over the world—Paris plus the Persian Gulf."

U.S. Air Force photo by Senior Airman Greg L. Davis

"Warthog" A-10

Nationally, 1,028 programs with a combined co-op student body of 200,000 are participating in co-op.

75th anniversary of co-op at UC
Close to 4,000 students participate in co-op, employed by 1,500 business and government concerns in 33 states, the District of Columbia and four foreign countries.

————— 1980 ————————————————— 1981 ————————————————— 1982 —————

TIME magazine's "Man of the Year" is the computer.

A Federal case

Look at the Federal Express logo. See the arrow created by the negative space between the capital "E" and the "x" of Express? Co-opping student John Lutz created that logo concept in 1994, and it was adopted by the company later that year.

Super co-op: When he says 'clean air,' he means it

In his 1996 co-op, urban planning major Nathan Meyer dressed up like an action hero complete with mask and cape for his employer, the Miami Valley Regional Planning Commission. He was "The Smoginator," battling for clean air through environmental education.

Co-op fun and games

"I worked for the Nerf team," says 2001 graduate Kevin Do of his four quarters with Hasbro Toy Group. One of his first assignments: testing the durability of Nerf guns and balls. He was told to take 20 Nerf balls and shoot each 1,000 times to test whether the balls became softer or maintained their firmness after repeated use. He also ascertained how the gun held up. "It was fun for about the first five hours. I did it for a whole week. I found the Nerf balls didn't soften after that much use. I also found that the gun shot better after continued use."

Quite fitting fashion co-ops

Maren Hartman co-opped with the HBO series *Sex and the City* in the spring of 2002 and for design houses that clothe celebrities. She helped design garments worn by singers Britney Spears, Diddy, Blu Cantrell and Eve on MTV, during awards ceremonies and for magazine shoots. Custom-fit co-ops like these didn't just fall into her sewing basket. Hartman literally pounded the pavement. While knocking at studio doors in Paris in December 2000, she remembers, "I got turned down over and over again, every time. One day, I was wearing high heels, carrying my portfolio and balancing an umbrella in the rain. I had quarter-sized blisters on my feet, and I just sat down on a step ready to cry." Realizing, as she sat, that it's necessary to be strong enough to hear "no" a million times, Hartman says, "I got up from the step. I started out again the next day—only in flatter shoes."

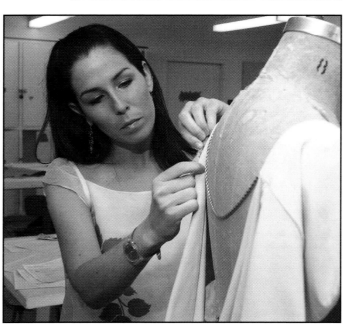

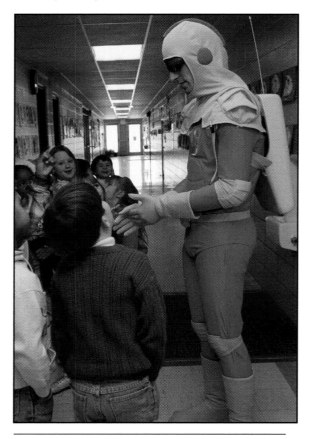

See the negative space created by the "E" and the "x" in the FedEx logo? That was created by UC co-opping student John Lutz. Other incredible co-op students include Maren Hartman, left, who co-opped with the HBO series *Sex and the City*, and Nathan Meyer, above, who played the role of "The Smoginator."

Above, left, is UC co-op student Shelby Shenkelman who met tennis great Todd Martin while co-opping with the Association of Tennis Professionals. Left is Jeannette Dehmer who co-opped for a year to help launch a historic space mission. And above, right, is Logan Allen who co-opped in Auroville, India, the furthest from UC any student has ever worked while on co-op.

Counting down to blast off

Aerospace's Jeannette Dehmer had a California co-op that was a dream come true—checking up on Albert Einstein's work by contributing to a historic space mission. In 2004, after 40 years of preparation, Gravity Probe-B was launched so scientists could measure how space and time are warped by the Earth's presence. Dehmer remained on co-op for an entire academic year to help prepare and test the satellite for its launch.

She knows the score

During summer 2003, business co-op student Shelby Shenkelman worked with the Association of Tennis Professionals (ATP), where she met the world's top tennis players, including Todd Martin. Updating match scores on the ATP Web site and reviewing pension plans for retiring players such as Pete Sampras had great perks. "During one tournament, Todd Martin walked in and said, 'Hi, I'm Todd Martin.' I was thinking, 'You're one of the world's top tennis players. I *know* who you are.'"

The furthest from home

The furthest from UC anyone's ever co-opped is Auroville, India. In late 2003, architecture student Logan Allen helped develop ways to use compressed-earth building materials for modern earthquake-resistant construction.

Golden Co-op Grads

On Target

Internationally acclaimed architect Michael Graves, '58, was mentored by his co-op employers—Carl Strauss and Roy Roush—long into his career, which has not only produced stellar buildings but stunning consumer products carried into almost every American home (by Target department store). "Strauss and Roush were great mentors and lifelong friends," says Graves. "I remember we all worked in one room during my co-ops. Carl allowed the co-op students to do so much. The more I worked, the more responsibility I was given." Graves has continued the co-op tradition in his own firm, and says no student has ever disappointed him in fulfilling a project commission.

Movie magic

Charlie Bailey, '71, has been creating special effects for countless movies—from *Star Wars* to *Pirates of the Caribbean*—at George Lucas' renowned Industrial Light & Magic. He's the most senior of a number of former UC co-op students now at work full time in Hollywood. Others include Scott Leberecht, a '94 industrial design grad.

Early co-ops had Leberecht literally crying to his mother, "I don't want to do this for the rest of my life." But a later co-op led him to where he really wanted to go: Hollywood. A Kenner Products Co. co-op making promotional toys for movies helped him to connect to the studios (who were Kenner's clients). Three days after graduation, Leberecht was working for Lucasfilm.

Diving right in

Co-op's founder Herman Schneider once said, "Another way to teach people to swim is by kicking them off the dock." Olympic diver Becky Ruehl, '00 grad in graphic design, seemingly took that advice to heart. The one-time co-op student finished fourth in the ten-meter platform dive in the 1996 Atlanta Olympics and won four national titles before she was docked at poolside by a shoulder injury.

Though Ruehl feels blessed because of her chance to participate in the Olympics and to win an NCAA title, she

George Kopp

At far left is Olympic diver and one-time UC co-op student Becky Ruehl. Near left is movie special-effects creator Charlie Bailey, also a former UC co-op student. Above is renowned architect Michael Graves, who continues the co-op tradition he learned at UC in his own firm.

says the best thing was the "incredible education" she received. "The education means more to me than any of the athletic stuff, because it will last my entire life." She also maintains her affection for the co-op program. "When we (students) came back together after co-ops, it was like having a bunch of people over and enjoying a big, central pot of food. You're all contributing to the pot and taking the most delicious parts out to eat. Co-op is that big bowl of food in the middle. When we came back together after co-op, it was a feast of information about resources, computer programs, ways to do projects."

Crowning achievement

Fashion co-op Heather French Henry, '97, went on to become Miss America 2000. Looking back, she says, "People always ask me how I prepared for Miss America. I always say, 'Five years of design school and co-op.' The lessons you learn last a lifetime. On co-op, you're dealing with CEOs of companies, companies that depend on you. You can't fail and come back next quarter. There is no 'next quarter.' These are real dollars, and they're betting on you." She adds that co-op made her fearless in interviews by the time she was competing for the Miss America crown.

And her crowning achievement as a co-op student? That came working for the J. Peterman Co. in Lexington when Henry, as a co-op student, led the company's move from hand illustrating to computer sketching. "I taught the whole staff how to do flat sketches on the computer, and so everyone got a couple of extra days off at Christmas because of the increased productivity." Much later, when interviewing for a job with the company, a staff member wanted to see how Henry performed with flat sketching on the computer. "I remember saying, 'I taught you how to do that.'"

Building laughter with the Hollywood stars

His co-ops led one-time architecture student Mike Gasaway to the realization that he'd rather do "kids' stuff" with his life. The architecture animations he did on co-op led him to a career in entertainment animation and directing. He's now the award-winning director of *The Adventures of Jimmy Neutron: Boy Genius*, named the Best Animated Television Series for Children in 2004. The show employs some of Hollywood's best comedic talent, including Mel Brooks and Tim Allen, as well as Christian Slater, all of whom have provided their voices to *Jimmy Neutron* characters. Gasaway says he'll never forget the day Mel Brooks ridiculed his name. "When Mel makes fun of your name, it has a whole different quality than what the kids at school did when I was growing up. I had to call my dad right away after receiving a ribbing from Mel."

B.V. Boyajian

Above is former UC co-op student and Miss America 2000 Heather French Henry. At right is cartoon character Jimmy Neutron, who is brought to life for television by director Mike Gasaway, who started his Hollywood animation career thanks to UC co-ops.

Co-op goes global

UC co-op student Mike Boczek, aerospace, '97, enjoys the sunset in Miyajima Island, Japan.

OH, THE PLACES THEY GO

To fashions at Hot Kiss
(Designed in L.A.)
And graphics for Wal-Mart
Dot-com in CA,
UC sends the co-ops
To work and to learn
And earn some good
paychecks
Before they return.

At Pratt and at Whitney
Aerospacers soar.
Accountants help Johnson
With numbers galore.
For co-ops in finance,
Americans smart,
But digi-designers
Love Hasbro Games' heart.

At Maui Tomorrow,
Urb-planners declare

That cool space is crucial
For neighborhoods fair.
Managers industr'l
To Florida trek
So lush Gecko Gardens
Won't turn out a wreck.

The marketing co-ops
To Nielsen parade;
Their temple of ratings
Is nobly arrayed.
Engineers industr'l
Work hard to ensure
Genteel Batesville Caskets
Forever endure.

To Claiborne and OshKosh,
Vic's Secret, the Gap,
Wild Flavors and Dow Chem,
They criss-cross the map.
For earning and learning,

Co-ops from UC
Leap oceans and mountains,
Shout "Ya" and "Mai oui!"

Their wonderful bosses,
Too many to tell,
All share in the brainwork
Of co-ops so swell.
Their talent and spirit
Expand what they learn,
Plus earn some good
paychecks
Before they return.

—*Mary Niehaus, with
apologies to Dr. Seuss*

> *"The distance is nothing; it's only the first step that is difficult."*
>
> —*Marie de Vichy-Chamrond, Marquise du Deffand, 1697–1780*
> *French noblewoman and literary figure*

Co-op goes global

OK, OK, the purists would say that we've *always* had international co-op ... and they'd be right. Almost from the first, students, educators and others trotted up from Chile or over from Ukraine and from points ranging from China to Uruguay to join in or testily probe UC's co-op program. Just as quickly, UC co-op students were off and working abroad, to Britain in the north and Brazil in the south.

But as the world grew smaller and smaller, it made sense to expand the co-op program so that UC students were steadily prepared and sturdily launched into career positions around the globe. What had been "international co-op on the fly," so to speak, became an established gateway of wider prospects for more and more students. In 1990, UC opened its International Co-op Program to continuously and deliberately prepare students to live and work abroad by means of intensive language and cultural preparation. Since then, about 1,200 students have worked abroad, mainly in Japan, Germany, Chile and Mexico but in other countries too: China, Costa Rica, France, Finland, Ireland, the Philippines, Portugal, Poland, India and Nepal.

The Neuschwanstein Castle, built by Mad King Ludwig near Innsbruck, Austria, as it was photographed by a UC co-op student at work in Germany.

International Co-op Program begins at UC.

The undergraduate medical technology program, part of UC's pathology and laboratory medicine department, goes co-op. This was the first co-op program at the Medical Center and one of only a few of its kind in the country.

◄———— 1986 ———————————————— 1990 ———————————————— 1991 ————►

The Cold War ends, and the U.S. is the world's only superpower.

After Iraq invades and occupies neighboring Kuwait, U.S. forces drive Iraq's forces from the country in the first Gulf War.

Benjamin "I think you can pick me out" Lang co-opped with Japan's Toyobo Co. in 1998. He liked it so much that he later returned to Japan to work as coordinator of international relations for the City of Iwamizawa. He's now living and working in Tokyo.

Photo Finnish

College of Applied Science co-op students David Zalar, left, and Paul Lesniak, right, display a newspaper clipping about themselves, written while they were each on a 1993 co-op in Finland. That co-op brought opportunities for yacht trips, a champagne bus tour of St. Petersburg and a tour of a school where faculty and students walked out for coffee breaks when lectures started to drag.

Co-ops abroad write home

In many workplaces across Bavaria, beer is allowed to be drunk anytime during the day and yes, sometimes for breakfast.

Lunch is the main meal of the day.

Everyone uses a knife and fork *always*. Eating a pizza without knife and fork is considered savage.

—**Matt Mickelson,** '03

Andrea Berning co-opped in Germany in 1996 and made a side trip to Catenhorn village in Rheine where her father's family once lived. "As a stranger in a small village, a lady stopped me and asked me if I was lost! I told her my family came from here, and I just wanted to look around a little. She asked me my name and pointed me in the direction of the family there with my last name. They invited me in, fed me lunch and invited me back again. They got out their family tree and pictures and figured out where our families fit together."

—**Andrea Berning,** '97

In 1996 co-op student Eric Knopp was the first international student working at Kawasaki Steel (in Chiba) who ever delivered his introductory speech in Japanese. "I cannot tell you how much respect this won for me. Everyone told me that my Japanese is the best of any foreign student they've ever had. That says a lot for the IEP (the UC preparation program)

because Kawasaki has been employing foreign students for at least three or four years and also hires students from Canada and France.

—**Eric Knopp,** '97

As part of a 2003 Web-development team in Chile, David Gash reported that Chilean working life was very similar to that in the States: "I still have to attend lots of meetings, except this time I have a better excuse for not understanding what's going on. And, no, I do not get to take a nap during the middle of the day, although sometimes my head does start to nod a little after a good lunch. And yes, the toilets do flush the other way in the Southern Hemisphere."

—**David Gash,** '04

I find it really exciting to look forward to my return to the U.S., to seeing how my experience affects my work. It will also be extremely interesting to see how I return to the environment in the States that I left behind because I sure am different. I am very motivated and eager about returning and planning the next venture, which very well may be turning around and coming right back.

—**Annelle Suszkiw,** '04, who is now living in Germany, working as a graphic designer

UC students on their international co-ops: Left, Eric Knopp in Japan, above, David Gash in Chile and top left, Annelle Suszkiw in Germany.

LIFE ABROAD THROUGH THE LENS OF UC CO-OP STUDENTS

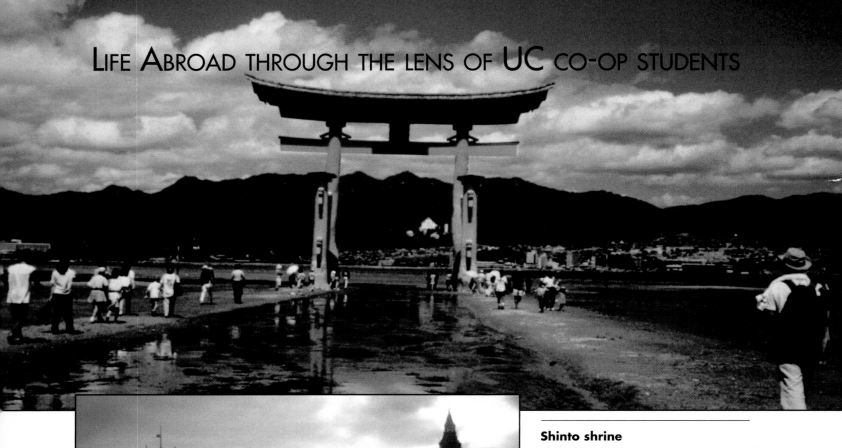

Kristine Killmeyer, electrical engineering, '98, at left, and Laurie Aktan, chemical engineering, '98, in London.

Shinto shrine

Itsukushima-jinja on Miyajima Island, not far from Hiroshima. In its present form, the shrine dates back to 1168, but there has been a shrine here from the sixth century.

Shannon Amrick, chemical engineering, '97, at the Rodin Museum, Paris.

Karthik Natarajan, chemical engineering, '99, in Paris.

A JOURNEY BEGINS

IN 1997, CIVIL ENGINEERING STUDENT Sarah Gray became the first UC co-op student placed with a firm in the former East Germany. She kept a journal of her experiences in Dresden and following is an excerpt:

When I boarded the train that took me from Koln to Dresden, I knew my journey would be amazing. I was going to literally travel from one side of the country to the other, going to go from West Germany to East Germany.

In Dusseldorf, an older man boarded the train and took his reserved seat directly across from me. I was still not very confident of my German skills, so I didn't go beyond saying, "Guten morgen" (good morning) to him. About an hour later, I pulled out my flash cards and began to study some words I knew would be important for my first day at work. He piped up and asked me what I was doing. I began to slowly tell him (in German, of course) that I was an American student headed to Dresden to work. He replied, "I was born in Dresden." For the next three hours, he basically told me the story of his life. I wish so very much today that I could have understood every word he said.

He was 6 years old when Dresden was fire-bombed during World War II. He told me he could still see the orange of the fire and the black of the smoke. He told me that the treasures of Dresden that were not destroyed by the Allied bombs were destroyed or taken by the Soviets.

As we approached the former East-West border, he began to tell me about the travel restrictions imposed by the Soviet regime. By this time in our journey, the man seemed quite keen to tell me everything. I had my map of Germany unfolded, and we found approximately where Hof (a former East-West border checkpoint) would be, even though it wasn't on my map. We gauged the time and distance. We were literally on a border watch.

During her co-op in Germany, Sarah Gray worked for a structural engineering/architectural firm, helping in the reconstruction of the Fruenkirche, a church that was the most famous structural victim of the 1945 fire bombing of Dresden. Because of the restoration work she did in Germany, Gray was "redirected," as she puts it, and went on to earn a graduate degree in historic preservation. Today, she's living and working in Toronto and still keeps in touch with her office mate in Dresden.

As we neared Hof, there began a high earthen embankment on either side of the tracks. We couldn't see beyond the tracks.

The man kept pacing back and forth from the window on our side of the train to the window on the other side of the car. "The border is coming soon," he would say. He began to get really nervous. He kept looking out the window, seemingly searching for something. It was if he were the "Man Without a Country" in Everett Hale's story of the same name.

When we saw the shiny west-bound tracks, he said almost sadly, "We must have already crossed the border because the tracks are new." The man got off the train in Leipzig, and I traveled the remaining two hours alone in the compartment. My perspectives, my expectations of Dresden and of living in the former East changed during the train ride. I began to feel a melancholy, a humbling. For the first time since arriving in Germany, I felt that I was really a foreigner, that I somehow could never "fit in," that I could never understand what it was like to live through Dresden's history.

When I got off the train in Dresden's Hauptbahnhof, I saw a Germany so very different from what I had seen during my first three weeks in West Germany—old rail cars; old, gray, dilapidated buildings. Sad and tired. Fenced in. Empty. I knew my German experience was going to be very different from the other UC students' experiences in the West. It opened a whole new world for me.

After that moment, I realized how lucky I was never to have seen a war in my own country, to have always had a house, a city, a state, a country. Free from restrictions. Free from fear. Free from borders.

Co-op 9/11:
"It's like New York is missing its two front teeth"

New York's Twin Towers before 9/11
Catherine Rooney, a co-op director from New Jersey,
laments, "When you sail out on the water now and look
back, it's like New York is missing its two front teeth."

> *"When you get into a tight place and everything goes against you, till it seems as though you could not hang on a minute longer, never give up then, for that is just the place and time when the tide will turn."*
>
> —*Harriet Beecher Stowe, 1811–1896*
> *American abolitionist and author*

Co-op 9/11:
"It's like New York is missing its two front teeth"

"I was in the subway, and my normal stop was right under the World Trade Center. I got off the train and was going up the stairs. Just as I was coming out of the train, I heard a loud boom. I thought it was strange to hear a big boom like that way down there. Then, these two ladies went running past me, and they were screaming, 'Don't go up there!' but I wasn't sure why."

That's how Kara Mealy, then a 21-year-old UC co-op student working for a New York City graphic design firm, begins her recollections of Sept. 11, 2001, a day she thought would be just like any other in her workplace right across the street from the Twin Towers.

Ironically, since she was directly beneath ground zero when hijacked American Airlines Flight 11 slammed into the World Trade Center at 8:45 a.m., Mealy was—at first—in the dark about events that morning. Her goal for much of that time was a frustrated one—simply pressing on, trying to get to work at Two Twelve Associates.

Unsure of what was happening, she tried to take the steps up to the trade center shopping mall. However, a security guard blocked the doors. He didn't enlighten Mealy about events, but told her only, "You can't go through here." Mealy then recalls, "So, my only way out of the subway was to ride to the next stop. That's what I did. I still didn't know what was happening."

Finally emerging onto street level a couple of blocks away from the towers, Mealy was committed to

Photo courtesy of Megan Heller, UC co-op student

New Yorkers wrote on and hung sheets in the days following 9/11, seeking information about and mourning those lost.

1998 ———————————————— 2000 ———————————————— 2001

The closest presidential election in decades leads to a legal tug-of-war over a manual recount in Florida. Eventually, the Supreme Court halts the recount, sealing a Republican win.

The biggest merger in the country's history occurs when America Online agrees to buy Time Warner, the nation's largest traditional media company, for $165 billion.

Race riots rock Cincinnati after an African American man is shot by a white police officer.

Terrorists fly jetliners into the Twin Towers of New York City's World Trade Center and the Pentagon. A fourth hijacked plane crashes 80 miles east of Pittsburgh.

simply making it to work even after she saw that the first tower had a huge hole in it. She recounts, "There were tons of emergency vehicles and so many sirens. Then, I heard another boom [when the second plane struck], and then, everyone was running toward me. I can't describe it. It was a heavy tide running toward me. Everyone was running from the towers. The only thing I could do was run with them. It was a state of complete panic. No one knew what was happening."

Mealy never did make it to work that day, but her co-op employer Michelle Cates, a '99 co-op grad of UC's graphic design program, did. In fact, Cates, a designer with Two Twelve Associates, arrived early on Sept. 11 and was in the office right across the street from the World Trade Center when the planes hit. "It was such a beautiful fall day, very clear," she muses. "Our building was a historic structure with exquisite detailing. It was undergoing renovation and work on the façade, so it was covered in scaffolding. I heard the loud crash, and I thought something had fallen from our roof because of the renovation work. I heard cars

screeching and people screaming."

The cars were screeching because not only debris but bodies from the first plane's impact were hitting the roads and cars. "It was raining people," states Catherine Rooney, a co-op director from a nearby school. She adds, "Taxi drivers and motorists didn't know what was happening. ... Suddenly, a body hits the car, and the driver thinks he's hit a pedestrian."

The confusion of that day continued. Cates and her colleagues next thought a bomb must have exploded. That's why her building across from the towers was quickly evacuated. Authorities feared that more bombs might be in the area. Like Mealy and other Manhattan workers, Cates became something of a refugee on the city's streets. In the meantime, when the second plane hit the 110-story World Trade Center, jet fuel and flaming debris showered Cates' and Mealy's workplace on the topmost floor of a building just across the street. Two Twelve's offices were devoured by the resulting blaze.

View of ground zero from destroyed north studio of co-op employer Two Twelve Associates, located just across the street from the World Trade Center.

"All of us office workers were streaming south away from the towers, toward Battery Park, which is the southernmost part of Manhattan," Cates says. "As I was walking, I recalled seeing a photo of one person's family laying on the sidewalk. It had floated down as part of the debris that was falling like black snow. That's a regret I think, that I didn't pick up that photo. I started to, but everything was happening at once. I was nervous and scared. So, instead, I hurried on ... but I'll never forget that photo lying there."

"A freight-train avalanche of dust" chased Cates. She adds, "It followed us over bridges. It followed the Staten Island Ferry out into the bay."

Hours later, Cates crossed the Brooklyn Bridge to her home. She remembers, "There were hundreds of people to help. People were giving out water, offering rides to take you home. They were asking if you were injured. Everyone was actively looking to help. They wanted so much just to help."

That included Cates' mother, a Cincinnati resident who was anxious to rescue her daughter. Cates states, "I called my mom to let her know I was safe. She told me right away, 'I can come in a car right now and get you! You name it. You tell me when.'"

Cates chose to remain in New York City, and UC co-op students—like Kara Mealy and a score of others—did return to work there as part of their co-op schedules after 9/11. As one co-op student, who arrived just two weeks afterward to begin working in New York, put it—"We might have come late, but we came."

"I KNOW WHERE HOME IS NOW."

ONE OF UC'S CO-OP FACULTY MEMBERS was all set to fly home to Cincinnati from Europe on Sept. 12, 2001. That didn't happen for Vasso Apostolides, associate professor, who says, "On Sept. 11, I was in Athens after having visited one of the Greek islands. I was set to return to the United States the next day. My mom called while I was in Athens, saying something about the Twin Towers. My mom is in her 90s, and I just figured she'd gotten mixed up so I said, 'No, Mom,

you can't be right. It must be some kind of military exercise.' She got mad and said, 'I'm not senile yet!'"

Apostolides, who came to live in the U.S. from Greece 34 years ago, admits that her forced layover in Greece during mid-September 2001 was a strain. "For the first time in my life, Greece seemed like a foreign land to me," she says. "I'd never felt that before. I felt like I was just stuck there."

"While I still have ties to Greece,

America is my home. When I finally arrived at the Cincinnati airport (on Sept. 20), the first sight to greet me was an official sign reading, 'Welcome to the United States.' A homemade sign was beneath the official one, reading, 'America welcomes you home.'

"I burst into tears when I saw that," Apostolides adds. "I couldn't help it. It was a powerful moment for me. I knew I was home. I may not have been born here, but I know where my home is now."

Vasso Apostolides

IT'S A GIVEN THAT UC'S CO-OP students in New York City at the time of 9/11 keenly felt the intestinal-level fear all around them that chaotic day. And working in Cincinnati, Erin McKinstry, then a 21-year-old marketing/management co-op student, felt the reverberations as the assistant manager at Cincinnati's Kings Island Resort and Conference Center.

As the summer was winding down, the conference center was hosting a Sept. 11 gathering of school principals and counselors. "Once the TV in the lobby switched over to Twin Towers coverage, there was chaos in our lobby. It was crazy," McKinstry recounts. "We saw the second plane hit, and everyone was finding a phone, gathering in clumps in the lobby, using standing phones and sharing cell phones because all the schools were going on lockdown, meaning no one could go into or come out of them."

What's worse, she adds, is that two of the counselors were sobbing, frantic because their husbands had been set to fly out of Boston that morning. (Both planes that struck the World Trade Center took off from Boston.) "They were desperate for information," Erin remembers. "What planes were their husbands on? How to contact them? We wanted to help ease and calm their fears, but how could we really? We didn't have that information, and then the second plane hit.

"It wasn't a conference anymore. It was confusion. The rest of the day just raced past in a blur."

She left work late that day emotionally exhausted. "I didn't know what to do to help those women. I felt so helpless. I never did find out which planes their husbands were on."

Now, looking back, McKinstry says she's a better person because of the responsibility she took on. She explains, "I was 21 years old that summer. But I'd been allowed to handle things as best I could, everything from 9/11 to a flood in the hotel when I was standing in about two inches of water behind the front desk. Now I see that I became much stronger because of that time and that co-op."

THE Cincinnati
POST
SCRIPPS HOWARD

➤ **Bush responds** PAGE 2A
➤ **Airport closed** PAGE 4A
➤ **At the scene** PAGE 8A
➤ **America prays** PAGE 1B

WEDNESDAY, SEPTEMBER 12, 2001 ■ Vol. 120 No. 219   METRO ■ 50 CENTS

TERROR

Evidence points to bin Laden

Associated Press

WASHINGTON - The FBI is using intelligence intercepts, last-minute cell-phone calls from jet-crash victims and search warrants to assemble early evidence linking the worst terrorist attacks on American soil to Saudi exile Osama bin Laden.

One investigative focus was in Florida, where agents sought search warrants amid evidence that suspected sympathizers of the accused terrorist were operating in the area, officials said.

"Everything is pointing in the direction of Osama bin Laden," said Sen. Orrin Hatch, the top Republican on the Senate Judiciary Committee.

Thousands were believed dead in New York and Washington, although an accurate count could take weeks. With a tragedy of such magnitude, investigators are moving quickly to determine blame. They caution it is too early to be certain, but they concur that early evidence points toward bin Laden.

Early evidence also suggested the attackers may have studied how to operate large aircraft and targeted transcontinental flights with large fuel supplies to ensure spectacular explosions - and maximum destruction.

A flight manifest from one of the ill-fated flights included the name of a suspected bin Laden supporter. Also, U.S. intelligence intercepted communications between bin Laden supporters discussing Tuesday's attacks on the World Trade Center in New York and the Pentagon, Hatch told the Associated Press.

"They have an intercept of some information that included people associated with bin Laden who acknowledged a couple of targets were hit," he said. Hatch declined to be

See **PROBE** on 7A

CHAO SOI CHEONG/Associated Press

Towers fall

➤ **8:45 a.m.** — American Flight 11 crashes into north tower of World Trade Center.

➤ **9:03 a.m.** — United Flight 175 crashes into south tower of World Trade Center.

➤ **9:31 a.m.** — In Florida, President Bush calls the crashes an "apparent terrorist attack on our country."

➤ **9:40 a.m.** — American Airlines Flight 77, carrying 64 people from Washington to Los Angeles, crashes into Pentagon. Trading on Wall Street called off.

➤ **9:48 a.m.** — The Capitol and West Wing of the White House are evacuated.

➤ **9:49 a.m.** — The Federal Aviation Administration bars aircraft takeoffs across the country. International flights in progress told to land in Canada.

➤ **9:50 a.m.** — Two World Trade Center - the south tower - collapses.

➤ **9:58 a.m.** — Emergency dispatcher in Pennsylvania receives call from a passen-

SUZANNE PLUNKETT/Associated Press

The second hijacked plane smashed into the remaining Trade Center tower and exploded in a ball of flame. Below pedestrians ran to escape the smoke and the debris. Witnesses were in shock.

DIANE BONDAREFF/Associated Press

Rescuers dig for victims in rubble

Attacks leave area in shock

By Barry M. Horstman
Post staff reporter

From gas lines and barricaded streets to a mayoral race reduced to an afterthought and a gnawing notion that life would never again seem quite so safe, the shock waves of Tuesday's terrorist attacks on New York City and the Pentagon engulfed a shaken Greater Cincinnati.

Like all of America, tri-staters reacted with horror and anger to the worst act of terrorism ever on U.S. soil – and

Every Season Is Growth:
Our Past Paving the Way to the Future

Above is fourth generation co-op student Amity Chaulk with a photo of her great-grandfather, Harry Pockras, who entered UC's co-op program in 1916.

You might say that Amity came to co-op by way of Mexico. In the summer after her freshman year, Amity went to Mexico—an educational trip paid for by her family. When she came back home, they were insistent that she get a job. That first, month-long job sold Amity on the value of experiential learning. She came back to UC for her second year, determined to take the co-op option in business.

Co-op rooted in the family tree:
2 families + 4 generations = 100 years of timeless training

"*You need* to get a job."

That's what UC finance and international business major Amity Chaulk heard from her parents late in the summer of 2002, after her first year at college.

Amity agreed easily enough. She'd lived it up with summer study in Mexico, and the start of school was a month away. It was high time to get down to earning some money.

So Amity went to work at the same store-fixture manufacturing firm where her father was an executive. "I worked in both the front office and the factory floor, doing everything from tracking invoices and doing bills to actually working with the store shelving and metal countertops we were producing," Amity explains. "I learned more in that month than I would have in a whole year of school. After that, I said to myself, 'I *have* to co-op.'"

Amity didn't know it, but she'd innocently forged the latest link in a co-op legacy stretching back four generations in her family, to her great-grandfather, Harry Pockras, who entered UC's engineering program in 1916. Harry was followed into the co-op program by both a son and grandson. And now,

some 90 years later, great-granddaughter Amity had branched out, opting for the co-op program in business.

Whereas her great-grandfather had co-opped for only one-month stints early in the last century (standard for UC students at that time), Amity's co-ops lasted six months each because she opted for "double-section" co-op experiences. (Today, a co-op quarter normally lasts three months, but students can elect to work six-month stints.)

With that first "double-dose" of work quarters, during which time she went to work for Marvin F. Poer & Company, Amity firmly rooted herself in the co-op tradition of living on her toes. Working for an international tax consulting firm was constant change, she says. "I never knew where I'd be next week or even the next day. I traveled to New Orleans, Mississippi and West Virginia. And you never knew quite what to expect when you were walking into company plants to assess the value and depreciation of their machinery, no matter how much research you'd done. When you go into a plant, there's often just a big mess of machinery. Co-op has taught me, 'Prepare for the worst,' just like the Girl Scouts did."

U.S. News & World Report ranks UC's co-op program as 4th in the nation.

UC's College of Allied Health Sciences begins co-op, as does the College of Nursing. Nursing becomes the first such program in the state with co-op.

According to DesignIntelligence magazine, employers across the nation cite UC's interior design and architecture programs as the nation's elite. Why? Co-op.

— 2002 — 2003 — 2004 —

The space shuttle *Columbia* disintegrates as it re-enters the Earth's atmosphere after a 16-day space mission.

The national World War II Memorial is dedicated in Washington, D.C., paying homage to the 16 million Americans who served in that war.

The world's most powerful earthquake in 40 years triggers massive tidal waves that slam into villages and seaside resorts across southern and souteast Asia. More than 150,000 die in 12 countries.

Amity Chaulk, December '05

Laurence Pockras Jr., '85

Larry M. Pockras, '51

Harry Pockras, '21

Amity is not the only "legacy" of four generations in co-op. So is Brian Binns, great-grandson of the very first co-op grad, George Binns of the class of 1911.

Ironically, Binns family lore has it that 100 years ago, George Binns' father thought the UC program was the *worst* possible choice for his son. It seems that George's father was furious upon learning that his son had detoured from plans to attend the Naval Academy at Annapolis in order to stay the course in landlocked Cincinnati. With time, however, George seemingly proved the soundness of co-op to his skeptical father. George's younger brother, Stanley, was allowed to follow in his older brother's wake and come into the co-op program just three years after George helped launch the experiment.

George likewise went on to bequest co-op to his own children. In the next generation, sons George Jr. and Jack Sr. passed through the co-op program, along with their sister, Audreana, the only girl in an engineering class of 75. Following in *their* footsteps came Jack Binns Jr., who passed through the program in the mid-1960s. He was followed, almost as a matter of course, by his own son, Brian, in the late 1990s.

Unlike Amity Chaulk, however, Brian deliberately factored co-op into his decision to attend UC in 1996. But

Brian Binns '01

Jack Binns Jr., '68

Jack Binns Sr., '40

George Binns entered in 1906, graduated in 1911

unlike his great-grandfather, Brian *did* give the U.S. Navy a try first. He actually went into the Navy for six years—only missing, as he puts it, the two land masses of Greenland and Antarctica in his worldwide travels. Recalls Brian, "I came out of the Navy in 1994 because I knew I wanted to continue my education. I looked at different schools all over. I even moved up to Seattle for six months to look at the University of Washington's interdisciplinary program, but UC was my best bet because I learn best with hands-on work. I didn't just choose UC because it was home for me."

In other words, co-op was a gangplank for Brian. He says

that just as the military educated him for one world, co-op put him on deck, educating him for the business world. "It was so worth it," he adds. "On co-op, I eventually held what was equivalent to a salaried position supervising and scheduling people at G.E. When I graduated, I stepped out of school straight into mid-level management [at a Virginia firm]."

And the next generation? "I'm the fourth-generation legacy. I have a real sense of pride about it," states Brian. "If I have kids, I'll absolutely recommend them to be the fifth-generation in co-op. It lets you stand solid on that first rung of experience before you grasp the second and third rungs."

Henry Ford had his Model T,
Herman Schneider his "Model C"

Top photo: The new Tangeman University Center, center, framed by the Joseph A. Steger Student Life Center on the right (home of UC's co-op offices) and the new recreation center at left.
Above: View of McMicken Hall through the windows of Tangeman University Center.

> *"The farther backward you can look, the farther forward you are likely to see."*
>
> —*Sir Winston Churchill, 1874–1965*
> *British statesman*

Henry Ford had his Model T,
Herman Schneider his "Model C"

It's no accident that Henry Ford stepped into his role as president of the Ford Motor Co. the very year that Herman Schneider pushed cooperative education to its stuttering start.

Both men were products of and catalysts for the same era of rapid industrialization. Amidst the tectonic economic and technological shifts of the time, both saw that essential overhauls—not just tinkering—were necessary in their respective fields. Thus, Ford devoted his early career to developing the transfer line that became the model for early-20th-century mass production. And Schneider sought to perfect what became the co-op model of industry-oriented education, the creative acquisition and deployment of applied knowledge. You might say that Ford provided fuel and Schneider oxygen to the expanding engine driving new concepts for work and learning.

Keen City of the West

It wasn't dumb luck that saw Cincinnati, long known as the Queen City of the West, become mother to the world's first cooperative-education system. The area had all the vital ingredients necessary to steer a new educational course—an abundance of manufacturing concerns, a well-established university and, importantly, a population where 65 percent were of German descent.

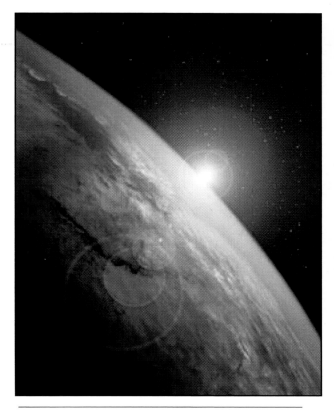

In 1906, 27 engineering students at UC piloted an uncertain experiment alternating time spent in school with professional work experience. Now, 100 years and 43 countries later, generations of students worldwide have followed our lead!

Again, U.S. News & World Report *lists the nation's best co-op schools. UC, once again, proves to be in the nation's top ten.*

Co-op turns 100!

For the seventh year in a row, employers nationwide name UC's interior design program as the country's best. They also name UC's architecture program as first among the Top Ten Most Innovative in the nation. In terms of overall quality, UC's architecture and industrial design programs are ranked No. 2 in the country. Co-op is a big part of the reason why.

2005

Hurricane Katrina descends on the Gulf Coast to devastating effect, killing more than 1,400 and slapping the region with more than $150 billion in total economic losses

2006

iPod sales sing. Around the world, 100 iPods are sold every minute, 24/7. Total units sold by early in the year: 42 million.

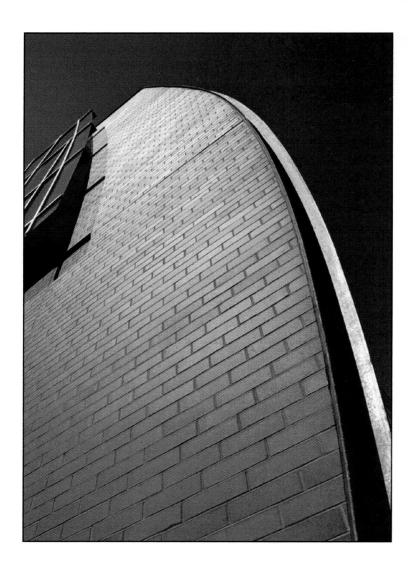

That German community, active in every aspect of the city's life, was familiar with the concept of European apprenticeships. It was open to adapting that Old World custom to New World and new-era needs to form a novel American solution—in this case, to meet objectives related to engineering education.

If co-op was to be invented anywhere, it had to be then-affluent Cincinnati, where the culture, the industrial resources and the educational structures all combined in a heady cocktail of development and experimentation. The only thing lacking was the ignition spark of one ardent individual with a red-hot idea.

The Co-op Bridge

Back in 1906, Herman Schneider came to a new town at the brimming of a new century where broad regional success required a well-educated workforce. In Cincinnati's then-accelerating machine-tool, turbine, packaging and banking industries, co-op was a remarkably adaptive tool for bridging

supply and demand in diverse professions.

Now it's 2006, and we're moving into the new century with expanding industries more often based on information and service rather than straightforward manufacturing. In our environment where increasing competition promotes specialization and where global challenges force all of us to focus on strategic advantages, UC is the premier cooperating partner to business.

For instance, UC was recently singled out by the Department of Education for a $1 million grant to continually assess the needs and best practices of 1,500 cutting-edge national companies and to make sure that co-op and the classroom meet their knowledge and skill demands. This UC model for real-time feedback quickly incorporated into classroom learning will be shared with co-op schools everywhere.

Here at UC, we will similarly stretch co-op's reach and its grasp in other ways. Our growth area lies in international cooperative education, co-op on multiple continents. We'll

UC's Engineering Research Center, home of the College of Engineering, the first college in the world to house a co-op program.

extend our presence in China, India, Eastern Europe and the Pacific Rim. Just as the expansion of industrial manufacturing is now outside U.S. borders, so too will be the coming increase of Schneider's cooperative plan of education. More than 1,200 UC students have co-opped abroad in the last ten years. In the next ten, we will boost that number fivefold.

And for good measure, we'll hone what we do here at home. Right now, we have academic programs—like interior design, architecture and industrial design—that combine first-rate national rankings with the opportunity for students to add to their education by working with great companies in all parts of the United States. It's a good mix, but we'll better it yet. We'll keenly attend to emerging markets, moving rapidly to target the hottest geographical markets anywhere on this continent. Tomorrow's Silicon Valley is where our students will be.

So yes, we will go out to industry nationally and globally, and we know that industry, in this century, will come to us. The recruiting of cooperative-education students is part of strategic-

Henry Ford had his Model T, Herman Schneider his "Model C"

hiring practices more and more common among employers. Because companies invest so much in a new employee, their ideal model involves meaningful testing of students *before* a final hire. And that's why UC and other co-op schools are drawing employers like magnets.

In our past 100 years, solid exposure to thousands of such employers has uniquely shaped the University of Cincinnati. It's a history of transformed students, changed lives.

And in that sense, the past century and the one that's coming are not at all different. So we need to do no more than look back to see our future: Cincinnati at the center. Not the Ivory Tower—not the Smokestack—but the bridge between.

UC's Joseph A. Steger Student Life Center, home to the university's co-op offices.